GCSE Coursework Series

Series Editors: Jon Nixon and Mike Watts

GCSE Coursework:
Religious Studies

A teachers' guide to organisation
and assessment

Dinah M. Hanlon

Senior Lecturer in Multicultural Education,
Christ Church College of Higher Education,
Canterbury
and
Adviser in Multicultural Education,
Kent Education Authority

MACMILLAN
EDUCATION

For Mary and Jim, my parents

The Author wishes to acknowledge all those who have contributed to the writing of this book. My special thanks go to the students and teachers of Mulberry School, Anne Parmenter for her special contribution, and Chris Dixie who discussed this book with me throughout its making.

First published 1987

Published by
MACMILLAN EDUCATION LTD
Houndmills, Basingstoke, Hampshire RG21 2XS
and London
Companies and representatives
throughout the world

Printed in Great Britain by
Vine & Gorfin Ltd
Exmouth
British Library Cataloguing in Publication Data
Hanlon, Dinah M.
Religious studies: teachers' guide to organisation
and assessment.—(GCSE coursework).
1. Religious education—Great Britain
2. General Certificate of Secondary Education
I. Title   II. Series
200'.7'1241   BV1470.G7
ISBN 0-333-45218-6

Contents

Editors' Preface

Coursework assessment is now a central feature of GCSE. It is a major component in almost all subjects for the six Examining Groups. Its significance is made clear in the national and subject criteria, and is endorsed by the Secondary Examinations Council in its 'Working Paper 2: Coursework Assessment in GCSE'. Under the old system, coursework sometimes featured in both CSE and O-level: much good and valuable work was achieved, for example, in O-level practical work and CSE mode 3 projects. However, the intentions behind the National Criteria make GCSE coursework quite different from what has gone before. Some element of coursework is now compulsory for all pupils.

CSE and O-level between them were originally designed to examine only 60% of sixteen-year-olds – at that point the least-able 40% were not to sit any examination at all. GCSE is intended to cater for all candidates and, in order to meet the needs of the whole ability range, has introduced the notion of differentiation. In principle this means that all candidates must be presented with tasks which they find manageable, satisfying and through which they can display positive achievement. Differentiated schemes of assessment are required of all subject areas – and of coursework too. That is, either the tasks set must be closely matched to learners' abilities and competences, or general tasks are set which are then differentiated by outcome – by what pupils actually do or how they perform. In practice, this combination of requirements can make coursework highly interesting and rewarding for the learner. It can also present difficulties of organisation and management for the teacher.

In many ways GCSE coursework seems more prescribed than CSE project work. The onus is now upon all teachers to structure tasks, to set and time them appropriately, and become invoved in their assessment and moderation. The purpose of this series is to help teachers tackle coursework within particular subject specialisms. The National Criteria define it as comprising 'all types of activity carried out by candidates during their course of study and assessed for examination purposes'. This means that teachers need to have a clear idea of the aims and objectives of their courses, and the role that coursework tasks play in what they are trying to achieve. The way that coursework is developed within music or drama, for example, will be different from that in science or technology. It is important, too, that the National Criteria say that the 'standards applied in the assessment of coursework must always be those which apply for the final examination, irrespective of when the coursework was actually completed or the assessment made'. That is, a piece of work handed in at the beginning of the fourth year must be judged by the same standards as work completed at the end of the fifth year. It means that teachers must have a clear idea of the quality of work associated with various levels of attainment at age sixteen so that they can gauge coursework at whatever stage in the course it is completed or assessed.

This series addresses the need of a range of subject areas. Each book follows a three-part structure – the first developing ideas and activities in the setting of tasks; the second consisting of a wide range of exemplars of pupils' work, and the third considering issues of assessment and moderation. Parts 1 and 3 serve to inform, raise issues and apply the more general points involved in coursework to each subject specialism. Part 2 consists of original pupil work – sometimes written, sometimes in other forms – and is used as the basis for comments in Part 3. Each author has attempted to address the many variations that still exist between Examination Boards and have attempted to take into account the needs of those teachers engaged in the production of mode 3 syllabuses.

In spite of this common format, the individual books in the series vary considerably. This is partly because the authors bring with them their own distinct perspectives and style; partly because the syllabuses across the various subject areas make very different demands on students and teachers, and partly because of the elusiveness of the term 'coursework'. The National Criteria definition is very broad and its interpretation varies considerably across Boards and subject areas. True, the coursework component is *usually* examined by the teacher and *mainly* undertaken in class, but beyond that there is little consensus as to what might constitute a coursework component.

On the whole, the books are addressed to individual teachers to help in the planning and development of their day-to-day work. However, the assessment of coursework may well depend upon the organisation of courses, and therefore be based upon group decisions or departmental organisation. We hope there is something of value here for groups and subject teams, as well as the lone class-teacher. It is important for all specialists to be aware of the work being carried out in other subject areas. As the boundaries between subjects become increasingly diffuse, we all need to be informed of developments in neighbouring subjects, and of their coursework and assessment needs.

No one can yet be an expert in GCSE coursework – at the moment we are all in the process of learning. As teachers become more practised in task-setting, recognising performance criteria, assessing coursework and undergoing moderation, the whole process will become easier and more familiar. This series is intended to ease the transition towards that stage.

Jon Nixon and Mike Watts

Introduction

One of Britain's greatest examination failures – Winston Churchill – had some reassuring words for those of us about to implement the new GCSE examination. He was once said to have commented that he would like to have been asked in examinations to display what he knew, instead of always being asked to display his ignorance.

The GCSE, with its shift in emphasis from measuring failure to assessing positive achievement, heralds the passing of the GCE and CSE examinations. Its major innovations are the introduction of a single system of examining all students, together with the introduction of national guidelines or criteria for each subject area. A form of assessment, with an emphasis upon what is practical and relevant, will partially or wholly replace written examinations. Continuous assessment or 'coursework' will be required as part of the assessment procedure in all subjects, including Religious Studies.

GCSE syllabuses in Religious Studies prescribe between 15% and 40% of the total marks to be allocated through coursework that is internally assessed by teachers. A significant part of the rationale behind this move is the assumption that coursework lends itself to the measurement of certain aspects of attainment not easily assessed through the terminal examination. In Religious Studies the exploration of ultimate questions might well be such an area.

Thus coursework is not something just to be tacked on to the end of a two-year course; it is an integral part of the main study, emphasising understanding and the application of knowledge rather than just factual recall.

GCSE Religious Studies presents teachers with both opportunities and challenges for which many, understandably, feel unprepared. This workbook is written to support teachers in their attempts to grapple with the major issues involved in organising, setting and assessing coursework in Religious Studies. It attempts to clarify the relationship between coursework and assessment objectives. In addition, examples of 'good' practice are presented, together with practical suggestions for implementing these in the classroom.

PART 1

1   Religious Studies and GCSE

GCSE represents a shift away from an 'examination-led curriculum. All syllabuses and examinations conform to National Criteria which were approved by Mark Carlisle when he was Secretary of State for Education. The National Criteria contain General Criteria referring to the ground rules for GCSE, and Subject-specific Criteria which provide the basis for the development of syllabuses and examinations within each subject area.

Religious Education

Over the last twenty or so years there has been a significant shift in emphasis in the content of and approach to Religious Education taught, both as a consequence of the 1944 Education Act and implemented through 'Agreed Syllabuses'. A broader 'phenomenological' approach to the study of world religions has largely replaced the 'confessional' study of Christianity. The phenomenological approach is seen by many to be the only means of enhancing the understanding of all students, as well as acknowledging the plurality of faiths in contemporary Britain. It aims to encourage an appreciation of the diverse and often conflicting life-stances and to give an understanding of the nature of belief and of the religious dimension of human experience.

GCSE clearly recognises the shift in emphasis from the traditional study and assessment of Christian Bible-based syllabuses towards the phenomenological approach to world religions, which includes religious responses to personal and social issues. The National Criteria acknowledge the curriculum development and good practice already in existence in common-core Religious Education. Consequently, amongst Examining Groups there is a wide and flexible choice of syllabuses and options within Religious Studies at GCSE (see Appendix, pages 73–76).

Aims of GCSE Religious Studies

The aims of Religious Studies within GCSE are presented in Figure 1 (page 8). GCSE emphasises that a religion (or religions) must be studied and explored as a living reality in the contemporary world. This includes topics such as the relationship between beliefs, values and universal human experience, and religious responses to moral issues.

Differentiation

Current examinations assess ability by means of 'discrimination', i.e. grades are applied as students fail to achieve a particular grade boundary. As the least-able students are said to have failed, such an approach obviously reinforces feelings of inadequacy. Such students are asked to display, as was Winston Churchill, their ignorance rather than their knowledge. Through differentiation, GCSE attempts to encourage the development and use of teaching styles which acknowledge and meet the needs of all students to achieve positively in the mixed-ability situation.

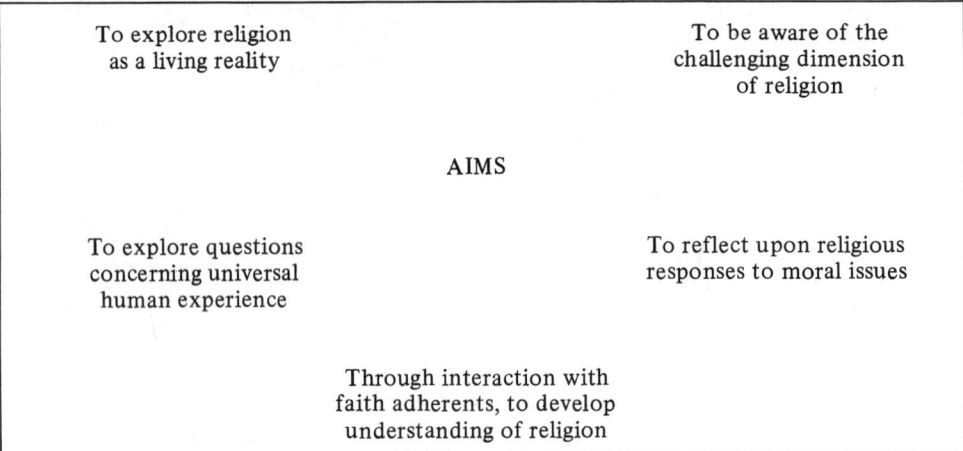

Figure 1   Summary of the aims of Religious Studies within GCSE

In order to award the appropriate grade to every student who reaches the required standard, teachers will have to prepare work for the mixed-ability classroom that enables all students to demonstrate what they are able to achieve positively. Differentiation within coursework is the responsibility of the class teacher, relying upon guidelines laid down in the syllabuses. During the two-year course, assignments will be collated in folders and marked internally by teachers in schools. The coursework will be moderated by external assessors according to national standards and regulated by the Secondary Examinations Council.

The advantages of devising tasks appropriate to students' individual levels of ability in order to achieve differentiation are clear, for teachers are in the best position to know their students, identify their weaknesses and strengths and design appropriate class- and coursework. In addition, coursework may remove the stress and nightmare some students experience with examinations and encourage a whole range of different responses which can be rewarded by the teacher. Coursework may thus reach parts that written examinations cannot.

Syllabus content

Syllabuses are drawn from the following major world religions: Buddhism, Christianity, Hinduism, Islam, Judaism and Sikhism, and can be studied either systematically or thematically. Examining Groups must ensure that one syllabus, under Mode 1 arrangements, is concerned with the study of Christianity.

Candidates will be examined in an area of content set out in either 4.1.1 or 4.1.2 of the Religious Studies National Criteria:

Either 4.1.1   (1) 50% A major world religion (to be studied through one or more of a variety of approaches)

                   (2) 50% Either (a) a major world religion different from (1) (to be studied through one or more of a variety of approaches)

                                    Or (b) the same major world religion as in (1) (studied through one or more approaches different from those used in (1))

Or   4.1.2   A thematic study of three major world religions.

Figure 2 on page 9 gives a general impression of the different syllabus options on offer across the six Examining Groups.

Syllabus Options	Examining Groups					
	LEAG	MEG	NEA	NISEC	SEG	WJEC
Buddhism	*		*		*	*
Christianity	*	*			*	*
Hinduism	*	*	*	*	*	*
Islam	*	*	*	*	*	*
Judaism	*	*	*	*	*	*
Sikhism	*	*	*		*	
Themes in Buddhism/Hinduism/Sikhism			*			
Themes in Christianity/Islam/Judaism	*		*			
Themes in 3 from 5 Religions C/H/I/J/S		*				
Themes in 3 from 6 Religions B/C/H/I/J/S					*	
Personal/Social Issues – Multi-Faith	*				*	
Jewish Scriptures	*					
Christianity: New Testament – Mark's/Luke's Gospel	*	*	*		*	
Christianity: Old Testament						*
Christian Perspectives on Bible	*			*		
Christianity: Modern Issues/Perspectives		*	*	*	*	*
Christianity: Roman Catholicism			*			

Figure 2   The range of content within Religious Studies at GCSE

Mode 2 and Mode 3

Mode 2 is a term applied to a syllabus which is internally devised by a school (or schools) and externally assessed by an Examining Group. Mode 3 is a term applied to a syllabus internally devised and assessed by a school (or schools), but externally moderated by an Examining Group. Whilst it may appear contrary to the 'spirit' of the National Criteria, both Mode 2 and Mode 3 syllabuses will be permitted, provided they conform to the General and Subject-specific Criteria. One of the important implications for Religious Studies is that alternative forms of assessment (such as assessment based on oral and practical work) can be incorporated.

Assessment objectives

The assessment objectives within the National Criteria fall into three key areas: Knowledge, Understanding and Evaluation (K, U and E). In contrast to present GCE and CSE examinations, greater emphasis is given to Understanding and Evaluation, which is further reflected in the coursework provision.

Paragraphs 3.1–3.3 of the Subject-specific Criteria describe the assessment objectives that must be applied to all syllabuses in Religious Studies.

Candidates should be able to:

(a) select and present factual information;

(b) show an understanding of these five key areas:
- ways of conveying meaning (language, terms and concepts)
- different forms of authority
- beliefs
- application of religious teachings
- exploration of ultimate questions;

(c) evaluate on the basis of evidence and reasoned argument.

Coursework

A major component of assessment of Knowledge, Understanding and Evaluation in all GCSE syllabuses is coursework. Simply expressed, coursework is all the work completed by students during their course which is to be used for assessment purposes. It represents a significant shift away from examination-based assessment towards centre-based or school assessment.

The inclusion of coursework rests upon the assumption that it is a reliable and valid form of assessment, able to provide both the flexibility needed to set appropriate tasks and a means of assessing across the whole ability range.

Grading

Grading is the process of identifying the levels of performance in assessment that will represent the different grades. Grade Criteria are statements which describe what students have to achieve in order to be awarded a particular grade. Within GCSE these criteria represent a shift from norm-referenced to criterion-referenced grading.

Activity 1   Background reading

In order to support this chapter and further identify what is new within Religious Studies at GCSE, teachers may find it useful to read some or all of the following:

1 *GCSE: The National Criteria* (DES)
2 *The National Criteria for Religious Studies* (DES)
3 *Religious Studies GCSE – A Guide for Teachers* (SEC and OU)
4 *Working Paper 1 – Differentiated Assessment in GCSE* (SEC)
5 *Working Paper 2 – Coursework Assessment in GCSE* (SEC)
6 GCSE Syllabuses for Religious Studies.

Activity 2   Points to consider

With a copy of the syllabus you have chosen (or are considering):

1 How does it draw upon your expertise and experience?
2 Will it meet the needs of your students?
3 Are you adequately resourced to teach it?

---

2   What is coursework?

Why coursework?

The General Criteria state that coursework assessment can be used to serve one or more of the following purposes:

(a) assessment of objectives not easily externally assessed;
(b) assessment of objectives different from those of a written component;
(c) assessment for which there is only ephemeral evidence;
(d) complementary assessment of a written component.

There are several benefits which arise for students, including the removal of some of the stresses of examinations. Coursework may also provide teachers with a vehicle for motivating students by means of more regular and immediate feedback and evaluation. Additionally, Religious Studies coursework may extend those opportunities for visiting faith communities and inviting speakers into the classroom, thus bringing religion into a more realistic context.

Most teachers of Religious Studies have always used a variety of teaching styles, including pupil-centred learning and project-work with its emphasis on individual research and discovery; activities which now fall within the scope of GCSE coursework.

Models of coursework in Religious Studies

Most coursework in Religious Studies appears to fall into one of two basic categories: small numbers of extended 'mini' projects or larger numbers of shorter assignments. The content of coursework assignments may or may not be examined in the terminal written paper – the coursework is said to be either integrated or extraneous.

Differentiation

A major tenet of GCSE is differentiation, and coursework is a means of achieving this. Strategies identified to encourage differentiation within GCSE include differentiation by 'outcome' and by 'stepping questions or tasks' (with an incline of difficulty). These strategies can be applied to achieve differentiation in coursework.

Rewarding positive achievement (which is central to GCSE) exposes a number of problems. For example, should the teacher be open about giving marks which will be very low, and if so, how will this help to motivate students? In stepped tasks will the fact that a substantial percentage of the task is out of the reach of the less-able student prove to be a valuable experience? Will this become more acute when students are placed under timed conditions? These issues must obviously have a bearing upon the teaching methods and learning approaches used in assessing across the ability range.

Coursework variables

Coursework can, and will, involve students in many activities and should result in varied outcomes. Some of the variables involved in assessment through coursework are presented in Figure 3 (page 12).

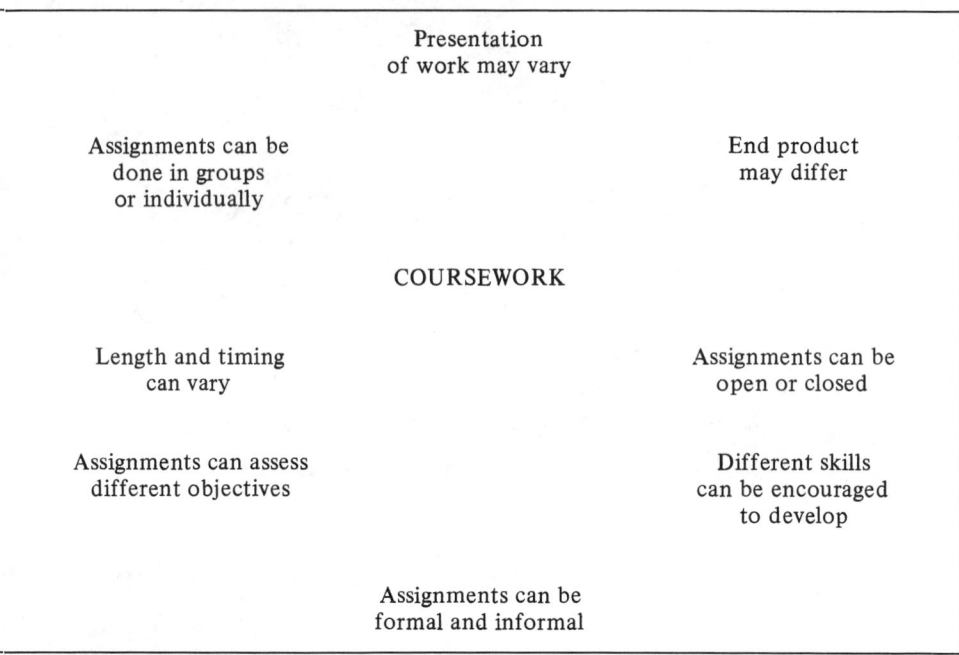

Figure 3 Coursework variables

Teachers must consider the variables within coursework assessment which differ across Examining Groups and might affect their choice of syllabus. Figure 4 (below) identifies a range of questions relevant to coursework assessment.

1 How many assignments are required?
2 How long are the assignments?
3 What types of coursework are allowed (test, essays, visits, etc.)?
4 What percentage of the total mark is the coursework?
5 What is the balance in coursework of the assessment objectives, K, U and E?
6 What is the balance between the assessment objectives K, U and E within the assignments?
7 Do students and/or teachers have an open choice of topics to be covered in the assignments?
8 Have coursework assignments been pre-selected?
9 Are assignments integrated or extraneous?
10 Are the resources adequate?
11 Can the department cope with the implicit marking load?
12 Does the Examining Group provide adequate marking and grading guidance?

Figure 4 Checklist of questions

Evaluation and GCSE Religious Studies

Implicit in recent thinking about Religious Studies is the principle that teachers should adopt an open or neutral approach to the teaching of world religions. Within their studies students will become aware that the world's religions differ from each other, in respect of the central beliefs and suggestions concerning practical living. An important assessment objective within GCSE Religious Studies is that students should be able to evaluate issues of belief and practice on the basis of evidence and argument.

Candidates undertaking assignments should be encouraged to be aware of the differences between religions in matters of belief and practice. They should also be asked to express opinions using arguments and evidence. All Examining

Groups stress that this element of the assessment objectives is in no way intended to test the validity of any viewpoint held by students. Rather, it is a means of assessing the extent to which students are able to support an opinion coherently.

Teachers will need to reassure parents that 'evaluation' does not require students to examine one tradition or religion on the basis of another. Evaluation will depend upon students' grasp of a religion and their ability to enter into 'dialogue'. Such dialogue cannot take place solely between teacher and students. It must mean that dialogue with religious people and communities has to form part of classroom practice.

Though this poses many practical and organisational difficulties, it will encourage greater understanding of the value of religious traditions. However, we have no desire to gloss over the concern which exists amongst many religious groups in relation to the philosophy of critical enquiry or critical openness. This important issue remains to be discussed so that these concerns and different emphases can be reconciled and met in the assessment of religions. Religious communities have an important role to play and it is evident that more teachers need to be recruited from religious minorities in order to transcend tokenism.

The relationship of assessment objectives within assignments

All Examining Groups provide information (and some degree of assistance) concerning the marking of coursework in relation to achievement of objectives K, U and E within the assignments. Each Examining Group specifies the weighting for each of the three objectives and how these objectives relate to individual assignments. One approach is that all three objectives are always assessed in each assignment, another is that only one objective is assessed in an individual assignment. It is also possible to identify a further approach which allows a degree of flexibility so that within an assignment any objective, or combination of objectives, may be assessed, provided that the overall relationship of the objectives is maintained.

What skills and abilities can be measured through coursework?

In the broadest sense the introduction of a compulsory coursework component within GCSE provides a wider range of opportunities for assessing those skills and abilities which are difficult to assess within the scope of a written examination. There follows a list of some of these skills and activities.

1 Setting students assignments which demand some *research* or *investigation* will enable them to order and process information, make them consider their evidence and encourage them to use a wide range of sources.
2 Allowing students to experiment with the presentation of their assignments may also involve them in developing *motor skills* when using photographic or recording equipment such as cameras, tape recorders and computers.
3 When a visitor speaks to a group of students about a religious experience students may be presented with a situation where they use the skill and ability *to think on their feet*.
4 Coursework can also be used to assess a student's thoughtful response to the study of a religious belief *orally*. This would be particularly helpful for those students who display insight, but are not always able to transfer their thoughts into sustained or exhaustive writing.
5 Working collaboratively with others in a *group* can support students to reach an informed view or opinion about a current social or moral issue. Working collaboratively in groups and responding to teachers and visitors can encourage students to develop valuable *interactional* skills.

6 Making and *recording accurate observations* during, for example, a visit to a religious building, can also be assessed through coursework.

The above skills and abilities have not been categorised in any way, but they may serve to indicate the range of assessment opportunities possible and the general benefits of coursework.

It is our opinion that the inclusion of coursework assessment moves thinking forward and away from the traditional preoccupation with what is publicly and terminally examinable. Not only will coursework take account of curriculum change but it should also embrace all that is best about mixed-ability Religious Studies teaching. It is therefore up to us, as teachers, to ensure that the end-product is of sufficient quality to attract students to these courses and that each student achieves his/her full potential in the subject. We must recognise our formative role and the unique contribution we can make.

Activity 3   Identifying problems and opportunities

1 Use the two columns below to list the problems and opportunities which you consider accompany the inclusion of coursework in the syllabus you have chosen.

(a) For you and your department:

Problems   Opportunities

(b) For your students:

Problems   Opportunities

2 In your opinion do the problems (a) for the teacher and (b) for the students outweigh the opportunities?

Activity 4   Coursework: making what is important measurable

A key aim in the introduction of coursework is to make what is important measurable, rather than to make what is measurable important. This activity asks you to consider the following points.

1 What is important in your approach to Religious Education/Studies in the lower school in relation to:
(a) your teaching methods;
(b) your classroom organisation;

   (c) teaching activities;
   (d) resources and materials?
2 Compare these with your current teaching practice in relation to examination groups, listing the major differences.
3 Explain to what extent these differences are due to the pressure of the examination.
4 Describe activities you might undertake with examination groups if these pressures were removed.
5 Try to relate these points to the aim of introducing coursework within GCSE.

3 Setting tasks across the ability range

Emphasising positive achievement

Coursework will have a marked effect upon teaching styles and classroom organisation. The traditional didactic approach will gradually be replaced as greater emphasis is placed upon a skills-orientated approach. Teachers will find the need to create opportunities for students to learn through practice and experience.

Coursework provides the flexibility needed to assess across a wide ability range. By presenting students with tasks or activities appropriate to their individual levels of ability, coursework allows them to show what they *can* do, thus emphasising achievement rather than failure. However, this is easier said than done, and teachers will need to employ a range of strategies if they are to achieve differentiation when setting assignments.

The effect of GCSE, and in particular the coursework component, on teaching styles and classroom management in the senior school cannot be overestimated. We have no desire to gloss over the very real difficulties involved in adapting to this new situation and note the genuine concern over the extra tasks now asked of the teacher, namely: reviewing of assessment objectives, identifying and setting appropriate coursework assignments across the full ability range and monitoring students' progress (see Figure 5, below). Success, it seems, will rest largely upon the type of coursework set.

OBJECTIVES
(What is being assessed)

SETTING TASKS

STRATEGIES
(Helping students positively
achieve objectives)

ASSESSMENT
(Have students achieved
objectives?)

Figure 5

One of the implications of the approach to task-setting described in Figure 5 (above) is that it cannot be separated from the assessment that will take place at the end of the assignment. We thus recommend that this book is read as a whole so as to include the points made about assessment contained in Part 3 (pages 53–72).

A major worry of many teachers is that within the coursework element they will have to set tasks that attempt to assess the Understanding and Evaluation objectives. That is, students must be allowed to demonstrate an understanding of a particular concept and be able to express a reasoned opinion. Coursework must do more than just enable students to recall factual knowledge, and teachers may wish to consider a wider perspective of starting points or stimuli from which to develop their coursework ideas.

To assist in this process we have included a number of suggestions in Figure 6 (below). This list is not meant to be seen as exhaustive, but shows that there are many possibilities other than just the more traditional assessment instruments.

Type of stimulus	Examples
Tests	The festival of Baisakhi The First Revelation to Muhammad The Passion Narrative
Essay	The extent of Jesus' power as shown in Mark's Gospel Islamic revival Hindu beliefs
Review	TV documentary on divorce The film *Gandhi* The video *The Silent Witness*
Research	Visit a Buddhist community in England Newspapers and magazines for problem pages on issues Interviewing a religious believer
Reports	A newspaper article on Bob Geldof and Band Aid A case-history A wedding ceremony
Letters	— to a friend about death and suffering — asking a Head for prayer-room facilities — about a recent pilgrimage
Imaginative writing	'Eyewitness accounts' – a Jew of Moses' day Dear Marge – advice-giving on problems and dilemmas Poems about war and peace
Biographical sketch	A day in the life of: — a person initiated into the Sikh Khalsa — Mother Teresa — a Buddhist
Surveys	— of a range of attitudes of people in your class — of the places of worship in the local area — of different versions of the Lord's Prayer
Art work	A model of a place of worship A poster depicting your ideas about apartheid and sport A newspaper featuring articles about a recent festival

Figure 6   Identifying a range of coursework assignments

Identifying the appropriate type of task

The problem of attempting to set tasks that enable assessment of Understanding and Evaluation is further complicated by the need to differentiate in a manner that allows for positive achievement. That is, students must be set tasks that are appropriate to their abilities. We now outline a number of different ways in which this can be achieved, although it is important to check carefully that any assessment method is allowed within the chosen Examining Group's syllabus.

Differentiation by outcome

Differentiation by outcome is achieved by giving all students the same neutral task. Teachers can then differentiate by assessing and identifying positive levels of achievement in students' outcomes.

For example, in order to assess whether students have understood key ideas about the resurrection of Jesus contained in the video *The Silent Witness*, they could all be asked to write a review to include, with reasons, their own opinions and ideas about the Christian views of life after death. Differentiation is achieved as students respond to the question at their own level of ability in their own review. In setting common tasks or using a neutral stimulus (such as a film, picture or diagram) teachers must ensure that the same meaning is conveyed across the whole ability and language range. Special attention must be given to the presentation of written and spoken instructions. If a short coursework assignment involves students in composing a letter to a friend in the role of a pilgrim who has just returned from Lourdes, teachers must ensure that all students in the class are aware of the conventions involved in letter-writing. This additionally involves teachers in supporting students to acquire study skills and in making extra provision where bilingual students, and those with special educational needs, form part of the GCSE group.

Differentiation using structured or stepped tasks

Structuring tasks in an ascending order of difficulty should provide opportunities for less-able students to succeed in the early part, and the most-able to achieve in all parts. In devising tasks, teachers need to emphasise their expectations for each student so as to remove feelings of inferiority and provide the appropriate challenge.

Within a mixed-ability situation teachers will be required on occasions to set different tasks with different levels of response. For example, students may be set slightly different tasks on a common project. Opportunities for this approach can be developed when a visiting speaker from a religious group is invited to talk. Teachers will be aware of the wealth of different tasks which could be developed – groups of students could be asked to research and devise questions on a whole range of subjects: one or two students could tape and interview the visitor; or the whole class could ask questions in turn. Facilitating a variety of interesting and stimulating activities may also enable the teacher to focus on a single student for specific assessment purposes.

Differentiation using group work

Group work is permitted by some Examining Groups and involves setting a task to a group of students in such a manner that each individual can be assessed as the task is carried out. Teachers will need to look carefully at how they structure group activities in order to promote active learning. Obviously many difficulties may arise when it comes to assessing the work of individual students. There is a need for careful documentation to ensure accurate assessment. The advice of the Examining Group should always be sought before embarking on adventurous group coursework tasks. Notwithstanding this, there are several advantages associated with group work, not least that it provides teachers with opportunities to observe individual students and helps bring assessment back into the classroom where it belongs. It also facilitates immediate feedback and allows tasks to be reappraised.

Activity 5   Looking at tasks

1 Listed below are some common classroom activities. Try to add at least ten more to the list.
   (a) Comprehension work
   (b) Discussion

(c) Drawing

(d) Reading with the class

(e) A class test

(f) Copying notes

2 Identify those activities you rely on most in your teaching. Do these activities tend to be:

(a) teacher-led;

(b) group work;

(c) whole class activities?

3 Identify those which you consider will actively engage all students in your class, encourage the development of religious understanding, and enable them to give thoughtful responses.

Activity 6   Differentiating tasks

1 Differentiation in coursework is aimed at positive achievement, not relative failure, across the ability range. Consider how far varying the language (including jargon), the style, and the form of presentation of questions creates different tasks, or makes the same tasks more or less accessible to different students.

2 How might varying the activities or varying the structure of the class encourage differentiation and positive achievement in a mixed-ability situation?

4   Organising and planning coursework

**Approaching the
two-year course**

When organising a two-year option course (usually for fourth- and fifth-year students) it is generally useful to break down the two years ending with the public examination into five terms, that is, a total of roughly forty-five to forty-eight weeks. Into this must be squeezed not only the traditional classroom teaching but all the extra work associated with coursework. We suspect that this will be totally unmanageable unless all aspects of the course are well thought-out and planned beforehand. This chapter attempts to outline the important factors that must be taken into account when considering and planning coursework.

**Implications of the
chosen syllabus**

Having chosen an Examining Group and with it a particular syllabus, the first step is to go through all the information that is issued about the syllabus by that Examining Group. The structure and requirements of the syllabus will have a considerable effect upon the structure and strategies of the course. The sections which follow list some of the implications that will stem from the syllabus.

Overall time allocation

Coursework is a means of assessment and thus it seems fair that the percentage of time spent on coursework during the course should reflect the percentage of the examination mark it is allocated. Given that many skills may have to be taught and that assessment of Understanding and Evaluation is time-consuming, we recommend that the percentage, denoting the proportion of coursework taken into the final examination mark, be taken as representing the minimum time to be spent upon coursework over the two years.

This may be increased if other factors are seen to be important. For example, if the coursework is extraneous, that is, taken from work extra to the terminal examination syllabus, the coursework component should include not only the assessment and the teaching of any necessary skills, but also time to introduce the topics themselves.

Thus, spelling it out, if 30% of the examination mark is taken up with coursework then we recommend that at least 30% of the teaching time, that is, around fourteen weeks, is devoted to coursework over the two years.

Number and type of
assignments

Given that students should not normally be expected to be working on more than one assignment at a time, the assignments will have to be spread out over the two-year period, spaced at sensible intervals. Other factors will obviously need to be taken into consideration, for example whether the assignment will require some form of student preparation or whether the assignment timetables of other subject areas will cause 'student overload' at critical times of the year.

As was mentioned on page 17 it is important to check whether the types of assignment tasks envisaged are allowed as assessment models by the Examining

Group. For example, a number of Examining Groups do not allow assessment via group work.

The model of assessment, with regard to the manner in which the assessment objectives are related to the assignments, may restrict the structuring of the course. For example, assessments involving the ability to evaluate and show a considered opinion would seem to be better not done immediately at the beginning of the course.

Method of assessment

It will probably save a great deal of duplication of effort if, from the outset, a scheme of record-keeping is adopted which includes, in the same format, all the information required by the Examining Group.

Teaching implications

Given that the teacher has adopted the spirit of the GCSE examination, this will have a number of implications upon the planning of the course. Some of the more important of these are outlined in the following sections. It is worth bearing in mind that as coursework is now an important part of the overall assessment, i.e. of the actual examination mark, teachers should realise their responsibility to organise this section of the course in such a way as to allow their students to show themselves to their fullest potential.

Teaching styles

Given that students will need to become more questioning and more able to research for themselves, teachers will have to be much less didactic in their approach. This underlines the need for teachers to provide plenty of opportunities in lessons for students to 'learn by doing', and to 'learn from each other'. As a general rule, teachers will have to minimise the amount of time given to the didactic approach, reserving it for the emphasising and clarifying of points between other activities.

It is always worthwhile for teachers to ask themselves whether there are other means or activities through which the teaching/learning can take place. Opportunities must be given for students to practise and rehearse those skills outlined in Figure 5 (page 16). It is highly probable that teachers may have to use a number of approaches within any given lesson and this in itself may be more demanding than using more traditional methods. However, the benefits to students will be great and teachers should be in a better position to carry out assessment as an integral part of lessons.

Resources

Teachers will need to consider whether they are adequately resourced to meet the demands of their chosen syllabus and should plan key activities and assignments so as to make the fullest use of the resources that are available within their department. However, in addition to this, departments need to review their resources (worksheets, textbooks, filmstrips, video etc.) to avoid obvious bias, stereotyping, racism and sexism, and to acknowledge cultural diversity.

A vital 'resource' for Religious Studies coursework is the arrangement of contacts with faith adherents and visits to places of worship, etc. Given the inherent difficulty of this type of activity, arrangements should be made well in advance. This would further enable the correct modules to be planned around what are key activities. (Further details are given on pages 24–28.)

Grouping

Given the implications within GCSE, teachers will expect students to work within a group for some of the time during coursework. It is worth bearing in mind that there are many different ways in which students can be grouped. For example:

(a) friendship;
(b) interest;
(c) gender;
(d) ability;
(e) for bilingual students: according to matched or mixed language level.

Numbers of students in a group can vary and groups can change according to the activity or task set.

Evaluation

Given the break from traditional teaching approaches it would seem to be sensible to plan to include within record-keeping some evaluation of the course itself. If, for example, students are expected to demonstrate what they understand critically, it is important to ensure that they have experienced an environment in which this could take place. A mere record of the syllabus would not be sufficient. This type of self-evaluation may be important within student profiling (see pages 65–66).

A modular approach

Given the nature of many of the Religious Studies syllabuses and of the assessment requirements, it is well worth considering the adoption of a modular approach to course-planning. By this we mean that the course-outline is broken down into manageable sections (say around four weeks' work), each of which deals with one particular subject area, topic or skill. The general rule is just to keep dividing until the modules are of manageable proportions without being too small or too large. Thus each coursework assignment becomes a module which may need to be preceded by one or more topic- or skill-based modules.

Not all topics or concepts can be encapsulated within a modular approach and, given a 'spiral curriculum' approach, there are a number of concepts that should be continually explored throughout the course. Perhaps the main advantage of the modular approach is that it makes the whole course manageable which, given the extra demands from the points of view of preparation and assessment, may make it possible to be successful in such a challenging area.

Activity 7 Number and type of coursework assignments

1 Do you consider that there is any relationship between giving students opportunities for positive achievement and the number of assignments they are given?
2 List the advantages and disadvantages of offering students (a) a range of smaller assignments and (b) fewer but longer assignments.

Activity 8 Planning to a structure

Using Figure 7 (page 23), organise a teaching unit and an appropriate coursework assignment from the syllabus you have chosen. A course can be planned starting from any of the positions.

```
                        What is to be
                      assessed (K, U, E)?


    How will I                                        What is my key
  group my students?                                    activity?

                          PLANNING


  What resources                                       How will I
    do I need?                                        assess the work?


                      What opportunities
                      are there to explore
                        and discuss?
```

Figure 7

Objectives (see pages 53–56) What information is required to ensure that students move towards an understanding and begin to explore the issues involved in the topic?

Activities (see pages 16–19) What activities are you providing for your students? There should be a range and they should be active and based on what is realistic in your situation.

Grouping How will you organise the class? Will you include group, pair or individual work?

Resources Ideally you should be aiming to give students first-hand experiences of living religions, but it is useful to remember that no single resource is indispensable.

Motivation, exploration and expression It is always necessary to stimulate students' interest by linking the work with what is familiar, and ensuring that there are sufficient opportunities for them to explore and investigate and express themselves in different forms.

Assessment (see pages 53–72) The assessment demands implicit within the unit should encourage differentiation and students must know exactly what is being asked of them in order that they can positively achieve.

5   Preparing and supporting students

Preparing the groundwork for assignments in lessons

With the emphasis upon helping and supporting students to achieve objectives within assignments, it will be necessary to develop understanding by drawing upon areas of experience, interest and enjoyment. Much of the groundwork for assignments will take place during lessons and the content of these will determine the extent to which skills and attitudes are developed so as to encourage students to question and evaluate. Thus, the work in the classroom must relate to the coursework assignments.

Encountering religion through dialogue

A glance back at Figure 5 (page 16) should convince teachers that many kinds of stimuli can be used as a basis for coursework. Encounters with religion, however, do not have to rely solely on secondary sources such as books or audio-visual aids. With an emphasis on relevance, GCSE Religious Studies should provide students with opportunities for meeting religious believers, talking face to face with them and visiting their places of worship. Encounters with 'live religion' will enable teachers to devise assignments which equip students with the knowledge and understanding of religious beliefs, actions, language and symbolism so that they are more able to make thoughtful, personal responses. We shall now look in more detail at practical assignments based on meetings between believers and visits outside the classroom.

The notion of commitment	The influence of the community	The relationship between beliefs and practice
Language and symbolism	**WITH VISITORS STUDENTS CAN EXPLORE**	Initiation rituals
Attitudes of believers to issues	Life in a community/group	The role of leaders

Figure 8 Assignments based on visiting speakers

Exploring religion through meeting religious believers

Figure 8 (above) gives some examples of possible stimuli that can be associated with outside visitors. Each of these can be used as a basis for assessing students' knowledge of a religion, their understanding of beliefs and their ideas and/or opinions. A variety of activities can then be developed for individual students, groups of students or the entire class. These activities should help explore the varied nature of religion, but preparation beforehand is vital.

For example, the teacher could organise:

(a) Group work to devise a series of questions for the visitor and the deciding of, for example, who will ask the questions;
(b) Other practical arrangements such as whether the session is to be recorded;
(c) The equipping of students with enough knowledge about the religion to enable them to follow what the speaker says. Research and reading can be delegated to individuals or groups on key concepts, major beliefs, etc.;
(d) The showing of a filmstrip, video or perhaps the reading of passages with the whole class, guiding students to investigate particular areas.

Exploring religion through visits

Figure 9 (below) gives some examples of various stimuli that can be associated with visits to places of worship. Whilst the assignments will define the nature and purpose of the visits, teachers should capitalise upon their use for assessment purposes. In addition to places of worship (church, mosque, gurdwara, synagogue, temple), visits to art galleries, museums, community centres and charitable organisations can also support coursework in Religious Studies.

To find out what happens during a service, ceremony or congregational worship		To meet and talk to religious people
To look at the main features, design and layout of the building	VISITS	To research into the history of the building in the local library
To explore symbolism in the building		To discover different uses of the building

Figure 9   Visits as a key activity for setting an assignment

Preparation is essential and includes: clarifying the purpose of the visit, giving the organisers information about the ages and abilities of the group, checking to see if cameras or tape recorders can be used and what clothing will be required.

Teachers can incorporate the following tasks:

(a) Identifying major features and symbols, so that, during the visit, students are more confident in asking relevant questions. This will ensure that their interest is engaged and that they are on the look-out for those aspects of particular use to them.
(b) Teaching with artefacts to familiarise students with religious objects associated with the building.
(c) Dividing students into groups to research for information on which to base their questions.

During the visit students could undertake a series of tasks, ranging through drawing ground-plans, taping conversations and taking photographs.

If students are to initiate their own meeting, visit or research, it is important to realise that they may need reminding about letter-writing, timing and overall organisation. Students should ensure that they include in a letter basic information such as:

(a) the purpose of the visit;
(b) the information they require;
(c) research and reading they have already undertaken;
(d) the people they have contacted.

Remember they will need to enclose an s.a.e. for a reply!

Parents

As already outlined, the increased emphasis in Religious Studies upon giving students first-hand experience of religion will necessitate visits to different places of worship and meetings with religious people and organisations. These can be stimulating and interesting experiences. It is worth emphasising to parents that on such educational visits, students go as observers rather than participants. Parents may wish to know about the formalities concerning dress and behaviour expected of students during a visit to a religious building. Further, it is worth considering extending invitations to the students' parents.

Classroom strategies with groups

We feel that relating coursework tasks within group work is an area in which many teachers will feel unsure of the best way to proceed. We therefore relate some suggestions associated with a sample assignment involving group work.

The purpose of the sample assignment is to assess students' *knowledge* of factual material encountered in the study of peace and conflict, their *understanding* of how people's attitudes to the use of force stems from their religious beliefs and their ability to make a *reasoned judgement* about the evidence concerning one aspect of the study *or to express a personal opinion* backed up by evidence and argument.

The assignment falls into three main parts:

(a) Knowledge: a written or oral summary on tape of the film *Gandhi*;
(b) Understanding: an account of a discussion between a pacifist and a non-pacifist;
(c) Evaluation: an essay about pacifism balancing all points of view, or an analysis of a survey in the local community or in the local church about attitudes to 'turning the other cheek'.

Students can be prepared for these activities during lessons by using the following work in groups.

1 A sequencing (ordering) task, working in small groups, on material which has a clearly-stated purpose, e.g. to order the major events in the life of Gandhi as depicted within the film. This activity will help students gather useful factual information about events in Gandhi's life and support their writing of a film summary.

Teachers would need to prepare a fact sheet on Gandhi's life which could be cut up (or rewritten) in paragraphs. Students are given between ten and fifteen minutes to discuss and rearrange the paragraphs in the order they feel to be correct. The finished results are discussed with the whole class when all the paragraphs have been correctly ordered. (NB: Teachers must ensure that they provide readers with enough information to work out the logical order of events and that key phrases or words have been used to help rather than hinder understanding.)

2 If students are expected to write or express their thoughts about issues, they must have opportunities to share their ideas. The following is an example of a structured group exercise used primarily to get students talking about war and peace in a general context, drawing upon their own experience.

(a) Divide the group into fours. Get each group to nominate a 'scribe' and a 'reporter'.

(b) Give each group a large sheet of paper with the words 'war' on one side and 'peace' on the other, and a large felt-tip pen.

(c) Ask each group to consider the meaning of the words and reasons for war and peace and get the scribe to write these on the paper.

(d) Give each group about ten minutes to work on this exercise.

(e) Ask the 'reporter' for each group to display and describe their responses.

In some cases it may be more useful for teachers to ask groups to undertake different activities which would contribute to an overall view of an issue. In the above case, groups could have worked on either 'war' or 'peace', rather than both.

3 A difficult text could be studied using group work. The text could be broken down into manageable parts and students, working in pairs, could discuss its meaning and report their views to the whole class.

4 Pictures and posters could be used as neutral stimuli for discussions between groups of students on topics such as peace, conflict, religious buildings, worship and beliefs.

Classroom materials

Hand-outs/fact-sheets can be used:

(a) to give essential information not easily accessible to students in another form;

(b) to provide students with examples of written structures;

(c) to reinforce oral work;

(d) to prepare sample questions.

OHP/wallcharts/boards can be used.

(a) to avoid lengthy teacher-input;

(b) to reinforce and display key points;

(c) for feedback and recording;

(d) to provide visual outlines to which reference can be made;

(e) to save time by preparation beforehand;

(f) to show examples of work you want students to produce, e.g. newspapers;

(g) to provide a visual impact.

The introduction of coursework will put teachers in the position of assessor. Teachers will be placed in a position in which they can assess more accurately if they support the needs of their students and identify teaching strategies to facilitate active experiential learning.

Activity 9 Introducing group work

Consider the following questions when organising group work.

1 Does your classroom facilitate group work? Is there enough space?

2 What task have you set? Are your instructions written or verbal? Are they clear and concise?

3 How is the seating arranged? Does the seating facilitate your task? Have you considered drawing a seating plan or keeping a record of where students sit?

4 Have you allocated roles such as 'scribes', 'reporters', 'leaders'? Are you ensuring that these roles are rotated?

5 Are the class familiar with working in groups? If not, you will need to introduce them gradually (in pairs, then fours, etc.) to these methods.

6 Is the task too ambitious for a class inexperienced with group work? If so,
start with tightly-structured pair-work with strict time-allocations for each
task and reporting back.

Activity 10   Reviewing your situation

1 Do you consider that any of the activities mentioned in this (or any other)
chapter are applicable to your own situation? If not, can you identify why
not and where the difficulties are located?

2 What activities can you devise that could form part of an assignment for
coursework assessment with your class?

PART 2 Examples of students' work

The aims outlined in the National Criteria for Religious Studies indicate a change in emphasis which will have a significant effect upon teaching methods. The emphasis on 'relevance' and 'what is worthwhile' will draw attention to the dimension of human experience within contemporary world religions. Students can explore this living dimension of religion through the study of beliefs, practices, values and attitudes as they are experienced by believers.

In this part of the book we present facsimilies of students' coursework (see Figure 10, below) so as to emphasise some of the points made on task-setting in Part 1 (pages 7–28) and on assessment in Part 3 (pages 53–72). Each example is accompanied by a brief discussion relating to the aims, assessment objectives and the nature of the task. Relevant annotations appear on the facsimile examples.

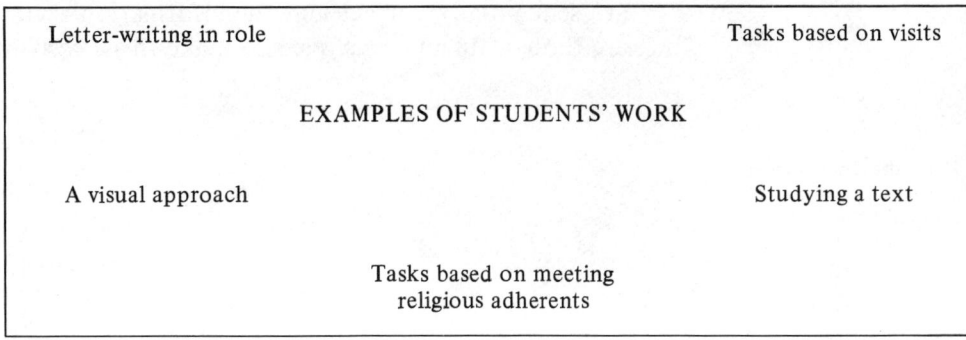

Letter-writing in role		Tasks based on visits
	EXAMPLES OF STUDENTS' WORK	
A visual approach		Studying a text
	Tasks based on meeting religious adherents	

Figure 10

1 Letter-writing in the role of a believer

An important aim in Religious Studies is to introduce students to the challenging and varied nature of religions by encouraging them to reflect on the underlying patterns of belief and religious practice. They should also be able to consider the importance of these relationships within the life of a religious believer. The ritual and experiential dimensions, i.e. the 'living faith' of a believer, is perhaps at the very heart of religion.

The broad aim within this assignment is to convey that a pilgrimage is a journey with a religious purpose, which may involve hardship, but is nonetheless undertaken with others as a statement of faith. In the context of Islam, Hajj (a pilgrimage to Mecca) is a 'duty' which all Muslims must perform once in their lives. The assignment promotes knowledge about Islamic beliefs by focusing on Hajj and by exploring key concepts such as 'obligation'. In addition, it aims to develop the student's sensitivity to the behaviour, attitudes and values of a life-stance with which they may not be familiar. Encouraging students to see things from the believer's point of view is an important part of Religious Studies teaching.

The assignment was introduced with a general discussion of holidays and travel. The specific content of Hajj was conveyed by showing a filmstrip describing the events of Hajj from the pilgrim's point of view. As well as being given factual information through map-reading and encouraged to research through textbooks, each student was given further opportunities to comprehend what happens during Hajj by participating in group discussions. Thus, the topic

29

involved a student in using such skills as listening, working together collaboratively, writing, participating in a discussion and creative art-work.

The student was asked to draw upon the information gathered and compose a letter in the role of a Muslim returning to England from Saudi Arabia after completing Hajj. The task enables the student to demonstrate knowledge about the beliefs, practices and key events associated with Hajj, as well as allowing him/her to demonstrate an understanding of the reasons why Muslims perform Hajj, by giving an account of what happened from the believer's point of view. This short task gives the student an opportunity to be assessed in all three objectives – Knowledge, Understanding and Evaluation.

A glance at the work will indicate that the feeling and atmosphere of the importance of the event has been captured: 'at last I thought here I was starting off on my longed for journey to Mecca' and 'my heart was filled with joy'. The student is able to articulate thoughts a Muslim might have and expresses these sensitively using correct terminology including 'Ihram' 'As-Safa and Al-Marwa', 'reciting' and 'tawaf'.

Within the style of the letter, and in the role of the pilgrim, the student demonstrates a confidence in writing, a knowledge of the main events and an understanding of the rituals associated with Hajj. The letter reads well, the facts are sequentially correct and the information accurate. The student's comments are thoughtful and sensitive and make this a convincing piece of writing.

The address puts the letter into an appropriate context →

112 ASHIKGONJ

12TH DHUL HIJJA

MEDINA

SAUDI ARABIA

Dear Saira

After a long wait at the airport I boaded the Saudi Arabian plane. When I got on I had a sudden feeling of happiness, at last I thought here I was starting off on my longed for journey to mecca. The plane landed at Jeddah there I donned the Ihram. I got on the bus to mecca, my

Awareness of the importance of the situation

heart was filled with joy the bus and coaches were filled to the brim it was a very tight squeeze but I didnt mind a bit.

Mecca is 72 kms away from Jeddah. The land between them is bear and desolate. It was quite a long way but it went quickly for me when we got to mecca. I went with the other pilgrims to visit the ka-aba in the Sacred mosque. we went around it seven times performing tawaf. There were thousands and thousands of pilgrims there. it was quite impossible for me to get close enough to the ka-aba to kiss the

Shows skill of empathy →

sacred black stone. I tried my hardest to get to the sacred stone but I couldnit, too many people had already got there and many more were in front of me trying to get there too. Then I went to drink the water from the nearby well I filled my bottle too so that I could get some of

the water home. I then ran seven times between the two
small hills As-Safa and Al-marwa reciting all the bits from
the Qur'an that I had memorised and learnt, I read my

Uses religious terms competently →

Qur'an all through the night. The next day all the pilgrims
and myself moved out of mecca to camp in tents in mina
there I read the Qur'an and taked   with some of the
other pilgrims. The Camps in mina were full with men

Accurate reference to the timing of the pilgrimage →

and women. on the ninth day of Dhul Hijja we moved
to mount Arafat. we all prayed from noon till after sunset
I prayed all through the night and read the Qur'an till
dawn at Al-muzdalifa a place near mount Arafat where
we stayed. the next day we all returned to mina to take
part in casting stones at the three stones which represent
the devil we prayed and remembered how Abraham res-

Sequence of events correct →

isted the devil. I then sacrificed a lamb. I hope you have
sacrificed an animal too. After completing Hajj I went
to see muhammad's tomb in medina. The grest mosque
in which the tomb is in is very beautiful. I also went
to see Hira cave were our prophet went to pray It is
very high up and steep.

　　　　Now this is the last day and I'll be coming
home soon after doing some shopping and buyinga
few souvenirs. give my love and regards to the family
I am well and happy. Don't worry and I'll be seeing
you soon.

　　　　　　yours sincerely,

　　　　　　　Hajji Sophia, Muhammad.

Maintains the 'role' to the end →

Example 1 A letter in role

2 Tasks based on visits

We emphasised in Part 1 (pages 7–28) that the coursework component within GCSE Religious Studies will allow teachers to take advantage of opportunities to introduce students to a wider range of activities for assessment purposes. The next two examples are based on visits to places of worship.

In organising and planning visits to places of worship teachers have an ideal opportunity to vary the tasks to suit the individual needs of students. Setting different tasks (see Figure 9, page 25) should facilitate differentiation, as well as softening the introduction of assessment to 'nervous' students. It will be necessary to devise mark schemes linked with each piece of work being assessed.

A A visit to a synagogue to observe a Bar Mitzvah rehearsal

The first example describes the importance of the Bar Mitzvah ceremony to the individual Jew, the Jewish family and the wider Jewish community. The assignment was made up of two activities. The first, a visit to a synagogue to observe the rehearsal; the second, interviewing some of the participants.

The task is specific, asking the student to 'give an account of what happens at a Bar Mitzvah and explain the importance of the ceremony for the believer'. Expressed in this way, it aims to assess the student's knowledge of the preparations for the ceremony and of the ceremony itself, as well as his/her understanding of the importance of the ceremony for all those involved. In GCSE terms, as the major emphases of this task are Knowledge and Understanding, there is a missed opportunity to assess the evaluative element. The task does not make it clear that a personal response is required and perhaps emphasises the need for the teacher to define tasks in relation to objectives.

The student clearly demonstrates an ability to recall factual information gained by observing the rehearsal. The relationship between the individual, family and wider community is considered: 'this shows that the father has released his responsibilities towards his son', 'For Lionel the Bar Mitzvah was very important', and 'He must have been feeling very nervous'.

A wide range of skills such as interactional (working with others), social (meeting and talking), and organising and processing of information which was collected through a recorded interview, have been used by the student. Teachers should support students and provide plenty of opportunities for oral work by practising interview technique in pairs, and asking the students to consider what sort of questions are needed to elicit the required responses.

Give an account of what happens at a Bar Mitzvah and explain the importance of the ceremony for the believer.

A Bar Mitzavah is a ceremony for Jewish boys. The age a boy must go through this ceremony is thirteen years and one day. This is the age a jewish boy is thought to reach manhood, according to the Mishnah which is a book of oral teachings written down in the second century ce. It has been a custom for a long time to mark this important date in their lives by this ceremony which takes place on the first Sabbath after the boys birthday.

The ceremony itself consists of three sections. They are the prayer of release, the message and the — festive meal. The prayer of release is called Baruch sephtarni and is read by the father of the Bar Mitzvah boy. This shows that the father has released his responsibilities towards his son. The service begins when the boy reads the traditional blessings and the Torah. He then reads the blessings

Incorrect spelling →

Has contextualised the ceremony →

Shows an awareness of the relationship between the ceremony and wider family commitment →

again to signify he has read the Torah.
The Maftir and the Haftorah is also
read. The message or the Bar Mitzvah
address is then given by the boy after
reading the Torah.

This contains a short message of thanks
to the rabbi and a promise that all
obligations will be fulfilled.

The festive meal is called Soudah
and ends the ceremony of Bar Mitzvah.
This is when gifts are given to the
boy. But nowadays the Bar Mitzvah
is said to have lost most of the
instructions required and only the
ceremony itself remains. Before the —
actual Bar Mitzvah there has to be a
rehersal so the boy can be able to
read the Torah and many other things.
During the rehersal the rabbi teaches
the boy what it's like to be a Jew.
He also teaches the boy to stand
up properly by the Bimah, which is a
raised platform used as a reading desk
usually in the centre of the synagogue,
and read aloud from the Torah.

Interesting personal
comments   →

A group from my class went to a
rehersal of a Bar Mitzvah in a synagogue called the North West Middlesex
reformed Synagogue. We went by train and
the synagogue was about ten minutes walk
away from the station. As we neared the
synagogue I noticed there was a cemetery
near by.

We walked into the purpose built Synagogue
and met the Rabbi, who sounded American,
and also met the boy who was to be
Bar Mitzvah and his parents. During the
rehersal other relatives came because
they were to take a major part in the

service. One cousin was given a new tie as a present.

While practising, Lionel (the boy) stood by the Biman, near the holy Ark, and read parts of the Torah which was numbered backwards. We noticed that he only read the Torah and did not sing from it. He used a yad to help him read the Torah which was in Hebrew and in English. There were no vowels or punctuations in what Adam was reading which made it very difficult to read. He seemed very confident while reading and had a lot of encouragement from the Rabbi, who cracked jokes, and encouraged the family to be relaxed. The rabbi also pointed out that a Bar-Mitzvah is not a theatrical performance

A salutory reminder ⟶ but a religious ceremony.

While practising Lionel wore his Yarmulke, which he kept in a small bag, and his tallith which he wore for the first time but found it very difficult to wear.

The Ark was covered by a blue curtain and there was a eternal light hanging called Ner Tamid, which was like a red light bulb. There were two menorah's, one on each side

Emphasis on position and ⟶ of the Ark and in it there were
importance of the Ark many scrolls, but only one was used. There was also two stain glass — windows in the synagogue and near the end grandmother arrived complete with "blintzes" pancakes, for the party.

At the rehersal we asked if we — could talk to Lionel about the Bar-

Indicates that the student
was well prepared
beforehand

Mitzvah. They said it was alright and
we could even use the tape recorder,
that we brought with us.

This is what was said when my
friend interviewed Lionel.

Q. When is your birthday?

A. March 14th

Q. Were you able to choose if you could
have your Bar Mitzvah?

A. No, it was already planned.

Q. Would you like to have chosen?

A. Yes

Q. How did you find learning Hebrew?

A. It was difficult at first but
once I got used to the main
letters it got quite easy.

Q. How did you prepare for your Bar
Mitzvah?

A. I started off with lessons for the
blessings and the Ten Commandments
then I went to have private —
lessons with a special teacher, once
a week.

Q. What are your feelings about saturday?

A. I am nervous and excited.

Whilst many questions were
generally weak this is perceptive
and would give insight into the
life of the believer

Q. What does being Jewish mean for
you?

A. Its a kind of way I call myself. I call myself Jewish so I

take a different standing from –
other people and I believe in
what Jewish people believe in.

An attempt to see things from the believer's perspective →

For Lionel the Bar Mitzvah was very
important and it could help him in
the future in his religion. He must
have been feeling very nervous just
as he said in the interview, and may-
be he went through this ceremony
to carry on the tradition of the family.
The Bar Mitzvah for Lionel showed he
was not scared to stand infront of
a lot of people and red aloud. For
me it meant I could go to an actual
Bar Mitzvah ceremony in a synagogue
and talk to a boy who has been
through one. I was also able to

Personal appreciation of the visit →

witness a Bar Mitzvah taking place in
front of my own eyes. I expected
the synagogue to be different from
what it was but what surprised me
was how much the whole family knew
about Judaism.

Example 2a   Observing a Bar Mitzvah rehearsal

B Personal response based on a visit to a mosque

The second example is by a student studying Islam who, as one of a group, visited a mosque, having been asked to describe its main features using diagrams and pictures as well as descriptive writing. All students on the visit were expected to carry out their own 'research'.

The visit encouraged students to realise that the design of a building, with its contents, reflects important religious beliefs. Seeing religious buildings and people at worship will help students understand religion and give them a rounded picture of religious beliefs in practice. Visits allow them to glimpse something of the meaning and significance of religion.

The visit was used as a basis for assessing the student's ability to relate the design of the mosque to Islamic beliefs and describe the visit in personal terms. As it is not possible to include the whole account, we have selected one page which indicates the student's knowledge and understanding of the mosque and its functions. This particular student gained a great deal from the visit and whilst giving a straightforward account, demonstrates a consideration of some complex issues such as the complaints of noise from the muezzin calling the faithful to prayer and a query about where the 'coffins' were kept.

On our visit to the mosque we were shown around by a caretaker. The mosque is the biggest and beautifulest mosque I have ever seen. Inside there were no decorations no chairs and no statues or pictures. There weren't any patterns either. The walls of the mosque were painted white. The dome was in blue, around the side of the dome it had the 99 holy names of Allah. They were written in calligraphy, with it small flowers were decorated with blue and green.

eg.

On our way into the main entrance of the mosque we noticed that the bricks were painted brown. On the front of the door thee is a big circle which has the word Allah written on it in Arabic. I have drawn a picture of it on the next page.

I have also drawn a picture of the dome. Every mosque has a dome on top of it. This one was very big round curve shaped with a little moon. It was gold with black stripes.

The dome

Before we could step into the mosque we had to take our shoes off and put them on the racks. We had to cover our heads as well.

Student shows awareness of conventions governing dress and behaviour in the Mosque

The mosque was very big. There were separate places for women and men to wash before prayers. The men and women pray in different places. There was a women's prayer hall upstairs and a mens downstairs. There were prayer mats on the carpet on the floor. This is to make sure that no-one pushes when prostrating. Prayers are held five times a day in the mosque but Jumma prayers on Friday are the most important.

Shows an awareness of different prayer-times →

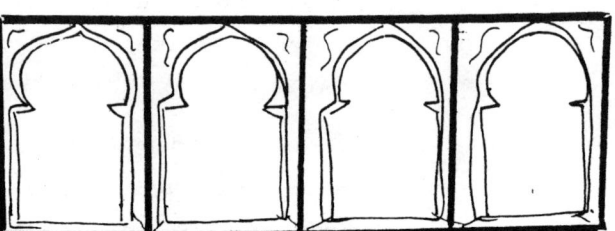

The carpet is like this, lots of small mats. When

Is able to identify and use language accurately →

Aware of who the leader of the mosque is →

Muslims pray they have to face the Ka'aba in Mecca. There is a qibla wall to tell them the direction of Mecca and the mats all face that way. The leader of the mosque the Imam spoke to us and showed us the minbar and mihrab. The mirab is the bit in the qibla wall to show where Mecca is. The minbar is the place where the imam leads the prayers from and is in the front. He uses a microphone. Also the Muezzin is the person who calls the people to pray and he uses a microphone too. There have been some complaints about this because of the noise.

Identifies an issue of 'religious' conflict →

A little weak – is able to identify other uses for mosque but does not expand →

The mosque is also used as a school for Muslim children to learn to read the Quran. The Qurans are on high shelves as a sign of respect. There are also other classes at the mosque just like an ordinary school.

We were able to ask the imam some questions which we had prepared in class. These are some of them. 1. When was the mosque built? 2. How much did it cost? 3. Where are the coffins kept? Also lots more.

An interesting and very human question which could be used to lead on to Muslim beliefs of death and judgement →

The mosque was built in 1980's and took two whole years and cost 2 million and a half pounds. The mosque is big for all the people to come and pray and read. We also asked the imam about the synagogue beside it and if there were any complaints between the Jewish people and the Muslims. No, they don't have any problems.

The visit was a useful learning experience →

Before we left the mosque we were able to visit the book shop where there were Islamic books, prayer mats and eid cards to buy. The imam gave our teacher a copy of the Quran written in Arabic and translated into English. This trip was very exciting and interesting and it has taught me a lot about mosques.

Example 2b Personal response based on a visit to the mosque

3 A visual approach

Interesting activities may encourage and motivate students, whilst varying the approach or presentation may promote active experiential learning. Teachers should be aware of the pitfalls in setting exciting tasks which fail to facilitate assessment of the Religious Studies objectives. On the other hand they should not be discouraged from experimenting, as many difficulties can be overcome by careful documentation and clarification of what it is that is being assessed.

In the next example a more 'creative' approach has been adopted by a teacher as a vehicle for assessing students' knowledge and understanding of the early experiences and teachings in the life of the founder of Buddhism.

The broad aim of the task is to motivate and support students who find sustained, or extended, writing difficult. It also attempts to provide immediate audio-visual feedback which can be shared. Students were asked to research for information in groups so as to 'devise a series of illustrations including maps, graphs, charts and drawings, together with writing, in order to create a tape-slide account of the early events in the life of Siddartha Gautama'. They were encouraged to consider the important events surrounding the birth, upbringing and 'enlightenment' of the Buddha.

In order to be able to reward students' positive achievement teachers must gear tasks to suit the ability range and needs of all students. Within past examination syllabuses assessment has tended to be used as a negative tool, i.e. students were 'marked down' for the things they did not know. The shift within GCSE requires teachers to look for and mark the things students 'can do'.

This task, like any task, is open to criticism, but it suggests that, to begin with, teachers and Examining Groups themselves will learn only by doing. The task attempts to convey the same meaning to all students and focuses on what they 'can do'. It has sufficient flexibility to allow students to respond to the activity at their own level and allows the teacher to differentiate by outcome.

As we read through this example we notice that the student demonstrates a simple (though accurate) understanding of the early life of Gautama. The use of pictures illustrates that whilst the student may not be able to handle religious language at a sophisticated level, he/she has understood quite abstract concepts such as 'enlightenment'. The pictures also indicate that the student has made some effort to research more than one reference book. Teachers must not automatically discount or devalue these responses, as it could be argued that the audio-visual approach has much potential within Religious Studies, not merely within the context of this example, but more realistically to record and photograph visits and interviews.

From your studies and private research devise a seriev of outline drawings together with a script for a tape and slide presentation on the life of Siddartha Gautama. Include the important events surrounding the birth, upbringing and enlightenment of the Buddha.

Slide 1   Siddartha Gautama - The Buddha.

Slide 2   Buddha was the founder of the religion know as Buddhim. He was given the name Sihhartha Gautama at birth.

Relevant factual
information
→ Slide 3   Siddartha Gautama was born in 563 BCE in north-east India at a place called Lumbini.

Slide 4   His father wanted him to be a ruler like he was and made sure that his son grew up in luxury. Siddartha was not allowed to leave the palace or to see the outside world.

Slide 5   He married Yasodhara and had a son Rahula. However, he was not satisfied and when he was about thirty years old he asked his charioteer to show him the countryside around the palace.

Slide 6   Siddartha left the palace without telling his father and had four strange experiences. First he saw an old man and then a sick man. He had never seen either of these before.

Awareness of the order of
events →

Use of map to identify and
emphasise the geographical
context

Express the idea of meditation

Conveys beliefs using symbols

Slide 7   He also saw a corpse, a dead person and finally he saw a holy man. He was amazed to learn that these different parts or stages of life.

Slide 8   Siddhartha decided to leave the palace to search for happiness and the meaning of why there was so much suffering in life. He gave all his wealth to the poor, cut his hair and led a very strict religious life. He sat under a Bodi tree to to meditate in the lotus position for seven days.

Identifies religious terms ——→

Slide 9   After some time he understood the 'truth' that everyone who was born would suffer, grow old, die and then be reborn. He saw that true happiness could only come when people got rid of their selfish desires.

Has reorganised information to express difficult concept ——→

Slide 10   He had gained enlightement.

Slide 11   From then on Siddartha Gautama was

called the 'Buddha' which means the
'enlightened one'. He had seen the light.

Slide 12.   The Buddha taught that eight thing were important these are mindfulness, effort, work,
action, speech, thoughts and feelings.
Understanding, and concentration. In Buddhism
eight equal spokes of a wheel represent
the eightfold path of the 'Middle way'.

A bit weak – mentions central belief but does not expand →

Example 3 A visual approach

4 Studying a text

In figure 2 (page 9) the range of syllabuses on offer at GCSE is outlined. These include the study of one or more of the major world religions viewed as a living tradition in the modern world, and based on the study of contemporary, personal, social and moral issues, as well as on the study of a religious text. Within GCSE, texts should not be studied in isolation from their role and importance for believers.

An essay

The first example is an essay based on the traditional study of St Luke's Gospel. A look at the heading indicates that it is testing knowledge and understanding of the Beatitudes, asking students to 'Explain the meaning of any three Beatitudes'. This essay, undertaken in timed conditions and without the text to hand, requires students to recall knowledge and information. When we look at the second part of the question we note that it asks students about the importance of the Beatitudes 'for the present day'. This attempts to elicit a personal opinion and a thoughtful response. Textual studies should be used to encourage students to develop their critical understanding and gain insight as to the significance of these texts in the lives of believers today. Once again, we note the need to specify assessment objectives in relation to the task.

Title reflects 'traditional' approach →

Explain the meaning of any three Beatitudes.
Show why these are important for the present day.

Appreciates the role and importance of the teaching →

St. Luke begins the sermon on the plain with a revolutionary set of beatitudes which provide a challenge to the individual. The word 'beatitude' means 'blessed' and they were used by Jesus to show his approval. They praised

Attempts to relate beliefs and values to the present →

what the world despises, thus giving a new meaning and set of values to a person's way of life, and because these are still relevant for the present day Jesus said: "How blest

Well expressed →

are the poor."

At the time of which these words were spoken Jesus could have been referring to either those lacking in material wealth or he could have been referring to the pious. The emphasis is on the word poor and shows that they are not neglected by God as society neglects them, and because of their lack of possessions entry into the kingdom of god, where there is real wealth, will if anything be easier.

Jesus continues to say, "How blest are those who mourn." He is not referring to some emotional and personal grief, but to those people who are distressed, by the amount of suffering and evil in the world as opposed to the amount of righteous and holy worship. These people are blest because they realise the fault of the world and are prepared to 'mourn' for it.

By emphasising "how blest are those who hunger." Jesus stresses his realisation of such a person's need can be overcome.

The messages are still important and perhaps more relevant for life today, because of the society in which we live. There are still extremes between the rich and the poorer people. There are those who do not need to work perhaps due to an inheritance or title. and there are those who even if they work everyday with Governmental aid can still not 'make ends meet'.

Interesting personal comments which show insight ⟶

The first and second beatitude are releveant to such poor people. In a society which stresses the importance of money and possessions, they must not despair. Their situation may seem to them totally undeserved and unfair. They must however, take comfort in the fact that while the richer people have had their time of prosperity, theirs is still to come in the cingdom of God, where it will be everlasting. This too must be a comfort for all those in need, whether a need of money, housing or food. Their need will eventually be rectified.

Interesting personal comments which show insight ⟶

In our society today there are many political and religious faults. There are those who recognise the irony of these. Holy wars are declared which in reality cover up a country's political motive.

There are many who are suspicious of Irav's religious leader and wonder if he is using the Muslim religion to disguise his political motives for the country to gain power. This realisation is recognised by Jesus who gives the 'sorrowful' hope in that 'their time of happiness will come', in the kingdom of God.

The beatitudes are a hope for those who find that in their society their status is despised. This will however, only be temporary and their future, one of happiness is assured.

Example 4a Studying a text: essay

A newspaper report

The second example, a newspaper report, allows consideration of what types of activities might be appropriate when preparing students for textual work. Here students were asked to consider the impact of Jesus as a miracle-worker and to discuss whether miracles still happen today. They undertook preparatory work in groups, being asked to compare and comment on Gospel accounts of healing and nature miracles. This group activity was followed by a look at present-day newspaper accounts of reported miracles. In order to assess their knowledge and understanding and give an opportunity for considering the implications, they were presented with two tasks: to write a newspaper report exploring the impact of miracles at the time of Jesus, and then give their own views on the implications of Jesus's miracles on Christians today.

The newspaper report aimed to assess knowledge of the Gospel account and students' understanding of the implications of Jesus's miracles on those at the time. The second task gave students an opportunity to reflect on the effect of miracles on Christian believers today.

The newspaper report follows the miracle in St Luke's Gospel, Chapter 9 v.10–17, though several inaccuracies suggest that the student was not very familiar with the account (e.g. 'the disciple Paul said'). However, if we look at the headlines, we see that the student does demonstrate knowledge of the impact of the miracle by his/her choice of words such as 'wonderful', and 'unbelievable'. Generally the piece is well constructed and reflects some knowledge of the text but the student does not appear to include a personal comment. This suggests the task is unfinished.

Daily Mail

6p (CHANNEL ISLANDS 7p)

MONEY MAIL TODAY

Wonderful! Amazing! Unbelivable! THE Latest miracle – performed by THE MAN proclaiming himself to BE Jesus!

Good use of headlines to create an impact →

(Col. 3) Presents wrong information →

Presents wrong information →

← (arrow to Col. 3)

Col. 1

This man–an Ordinary looking person in his Thirties performed a unique miracle far beyond the Capabilities or explanation of a ordinary man. At 11.45 am ← yesterday morning this man, claiming to be Jesus, went with his 12 – "duociples" to a town called Bethsaida. A crowd of about two Thousand people followed him

Col. 2

picking up about a Thousand on The way. They shouted and raved to people nearby That they were 'going to see Jesus'. Jesus welcomed Them and spoke to them about The kingdom of God. He also seemed to heal a dozen people of various illness. ... Including an old man who had been blind for thirty years. He talked to thim all afternoon and as

Col. 3

The Sun began to set. The diziple Paul Said "send the people away So that they Can go to the villages and farms round there and find food and Lodging because This is a lonely place." Then this Jesus replied 'you give them Something to eat yourselues'. I thought this a ridiculous request as by now about five thousand people had gathered In the town to Listen

↑ Content rather weak – does not expand ideas

to this man As well as this there were only five loaves and 2 fish to eat. Jesus made the people sit down in groups of about fifty each. Then he performed an unbelievable miracle. He took the five loaves and two fish, looked up to the sky, Thanked God for them, broke Them and gave them to eight of his disciples to distribute them to the people The amazing thing was that they ate and had enough and the other four disciples Collected up, twelve baskets of Left overs A true miracle and yet another action which may lead us All to believe	that this Jesus is exactly who he claims to be.	
Col. 4	Col. 5	

Attempt to relate the miracle to a belief-response ⟶

Example 4b Studying a text: newspaper report

5 Work on a talk by a religious adherent

Providing imaginative stimuli for students makes task-setting and assessment of coursework easier. Inviting a member of a religious community into the classroom can enable students to gain an insight into the life of a believer and find out the reasons why people become members of such communities, how they go about it and what demands it makes on their lives. In Figure 9 (page 25) we listed some ideas for coursework assessment based on dialogue with a visitor. The next example, on Sikhism, gave students an opportunity to listen to a talk by a member of staff who was also a member of the Sikh Khalsa. In addition, small groups of students were able to interview him.

To prepare for the talk and the interviews the students were given an opportunity to devise questions and practise interviewing. They were guided on note-making and encouraged to ask questions which would give them an accurate picture of the life of a religious believer. The following questions, for example, were produced by a group of four students to find out more about the Amrit ceremony.

1 What is an Amrit ceremony?
2 Why did you decide to go through the ceremony?
3 How old were you when you made that decision?
4 Who else was involved?
5 How did you prepare yourself?
6 What did you have to do?
7 Do women go through the ceremony?
8 Did you have to wear anything special?
9 Were there any special celebrations?
10 Has it affected the way you live?
11 What does it mean to you to be a member of the Khalsa?
12 Is the Amrit ceremony an important part of Sikhism?

As a consequence of the meeting with the religious adherent the students were asked to 'Describe what happens at an Amrit ceremony at which a Sikh becomes a member of the Khalsa' and 'Explain what you think is the significance of this ceremony for a Sikh'. This task required Knowledge, Understanding and Evaluation and was used as a means of assessing all three.

In the example, the student uses the questions outlined above to organise and integrate the information into an essay. There is considerable evidence of the student's sensitivity in handling the information gained from the speaker: for example, 'I enjoyed our talk with Mr Singh and I could tell that he felt very motivated towards his religion'. The student appears confident in handling religious language and includes several extracts from the Sikh Scriptures as they relate to the ceremony: for example, 'Wahe Guru ji Ka Khalsa' is explained as meaning 'the Khalsa is the chosen of God'.

"Describe what happens at an Amrit Ceremony at which a Sikh becomes a member of the Khalsa. Explain what you think is the significance of this ceremony for a Sikh."

I have not witnessed an Amrit ceremony because I am not a Sikh but in our RS lesson Mr Singh the Geography teacher came to talk to us. I learnt a lot about Sikhism and about the ceremony from him and from my own reading.

Uses essay title to structure writing and integrate own ideas and thoughts →

An Amrit ceremony is when a Sikh becomes a member of the Khalsa. They have to make sure that they can fulfil all the religious principles and live according to the Sikh Code of Conduct. Both men and women can go through this ceremony because in Sikhism all people are equal. Guru Gobind Singh

Well expressed – uses language and terms correctly →

instituted the Khalsa in 1699 at Anandpur. The
Khalsa was an army formed to protect Sikhism
from the oppressive Muslim rulers of that time.

Shows sensitivity and appreciation in handling the information →

Mr Singh decided to become a member of the Khalsa
when he was thirty-five years old. He thought
that his devotion to his religion would not be
complete without becoming a Khalsa Sikh.
He prepared himself for the ceremony by bathing
and washing his hair.

Awareness that beliefs affect daily life and that they appeal to religious authority, God →

Mr Singh wears a turban because his hair
must not be cut as this demonstrates his
loyalty to God. Kesh is the name given to
this and is one of the five K's which all Sikhs
must obey. The other K's are the Kangha comb
which helps keep the long hair in place and is a
symbol for discipline. Kaccha are white shorts
worn under ordinary clothes which replaced
the long loose garment worn by Hindus the
'dhoti.' These shorts represent spiritual
freedom as Sikhs gave up traditional Hindu
ideas. Kara is the wearing of a steel bracelet
on the right wrist and is a symbol of strength
and unity of the Sikh brotherhood. It reminds
them of their loyalty to their faith. The Kirpan
is a sword which is a symbol of authority and
justice. It reminds Sikhs that they must be
prepared to fight for God and defend and truth.
It is not permitted for Sikhs to carry swords
in Britain so Mr Singh has to wear a tiny blade in his
comb instead.

Kesh

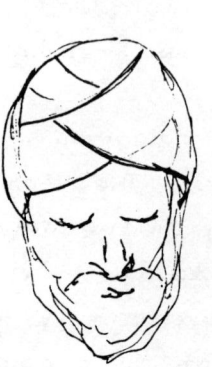

Kara

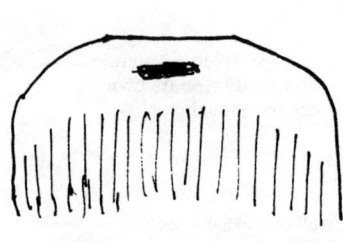

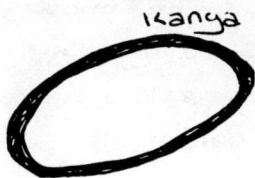

Kanga

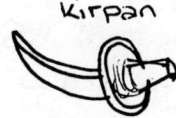

Kirpan

Kaccha

There were many other people involved in the Amrit ceremony when Mr Singh went through it. Five Sikhs called Pani Pyarees helped him. They represented the first five Khalsa Sikhs baptised by Guru Gobind Singh.

At the beginning of the ceremony Sikhs have to explain all the rules of the community. They must love God, read and study the Guru Granth Sahib the Sikh holy scriptures and serve people. Several passages were read from the Granth and amrit was made in a large iron bowl. Amrit is made from water sweetened with sugar and stirred by a large double edged sword called a Khanda. A senior Sikh read the Japji the famous poem by Guru Nanak, then a poem called the Jap Sahib is read. Everyone reads while the Amrit is being stirred. This ends with the reading of the Anand the evening prayer. After this the baptism took place. It happens like this. First the person is given nectar to drink. Then nectar is sprinkled five times into their eyes, hair and hands. While this happens the Pani Pyarees say these words: "Wahe Guru ji Ka Khalsa" which means 'the Khalsa is the chosen of God'. The person who is being initiated replies "Wahe Guru ji ki fateh" which means 'Victory to God.' At the end of the ceremony everyone who is present in the Gurdwara sat down and ate Kara Prashad

Good reference to the role and use of scriptures within the ceremony ⟶

together to show that they were all equal. It was during this ceremony that Mr Singh got his extra name of 'Singh' which means 'lion'. Women are given the 'Kaur' which means 'princess'.

Indicates some understanding and awareness of the way in which the believer's life has been changed by the experience →

I think that this ceremony is important for Sikhs because Mr Singh said that he was very Privileged to be taking the khalsa. It has changed his life because he does not cut his hair or use drugs or smoke or drink alcohol. A Khalsa Sikh is prepared to stand up for their faith and obey all the obligations of their religion. Not all Sikhs are members of the Khalsa but for those who are it is a significant part of their faith.

Direct positive evaluation of the talk →

I enjoyed our talk with Mr Singh and I could tell that he felt very motivated towards his religion. He was very helpful and answered all the questions from our class clearly.

Example 5 Work based on a talk by a religious adherent

PART 3

1   What does coursework assessment involve?

Coursework, as defined in the National Criteria for Religious Studies, assesses the extent to which students demonstrate an ability to select and present factual information, show an understanding of key issues and evaluate and express opinions on the basis of evidence. Coursework assessment may involve any combination of short-answer questions, structured questions, reviews, essays, comparisons of texts, project work based on visits, art-work and oral contributions.

In some syllabuses coursework assignments are seen as a parallel form of assessment, often having the same weighting of objectives as the terminal examination. In others, coursework assignments do not reflect the objectives of the terminal examination. Here, Understanding and Evaluation are usually weighted higher in the coursework than in the written paper.

Assessment objectives

Assessment objectives in GCSE Religious Studies test the extent to which students are able to show what they know, what they understand and what they are able to evaluate on the basis of argument. Explicitly:

Knowledge   Candidates must be able to select and present relevant factual information in an organised manner.

Understanding   Candidates must show an understanding of:
language, terms and concepts used in religion;
the role and importance in religion of special people, writings and traditions;
principle beliefs, their meaning and ways in which beliefs are related to practice;
religious and appropriate non-religious responses to contemporary moral issues, both personal and social;
questions about the meaning of life and variety of faith-responses given to them.

Evaluation   Candidates must be able to evaluate on the basis of evidence and argument, issues of belief and practice arising from the study of religion.

There are variations amongst the Examining Groups and syllabuses concerning coursework-weighting, the number of assignments and the relationship of the assignments to the objectives. In Figure 11 (page 54) we identify these across the Examining Groups.

		Knowledge	Understanding	Evaluation	Total %
LEAG		12	20	8	40
MEG		6	6	8	20
	or	8	12	10	30
	or	14	1·5	11	40
NEA		6	11	8	25
	or	14	16	10	40
NISEC		5	15	10	30
SEG		5	15	5	25
WJEC		10	10	10	30

Figure 11

It is worth noting the differences in Figure 11 (above) which exist between Examining Groups in relation to:

(a) the total percentage mark for the coursework;
(b) the weightings of the three assessment objectives;
(c) the increased emphasis given to Understanding and Evaluation.

In Figure 12 (below) we note the weightings given to coursework in relation to the number of assignments required for assessment by each of the Examining Groups. This chart raises several questions for discussion. Are the needs of students within the mixed-ability situation best met through the assessment of a smaller number of long assignments or a larger number of short assignments? A larger number of short assignments might provide students with more opportunity for the assessment of positive achievement throughout the two years of study, but this raises the issue of whether coursework assessment is to be a 'developmental' assessment. Fewer, longer assignments could allow students to demonstrate greater maturity, and a judicious selection of coursework might allow assessment to take place in the second year of the course.

Exam group	Coursework models (Number of assignments)	Overall weighting
LEAG	10	40%
MEG	3 3 6 4	20% 20% 40% 30%
NEA	2, 4 or 6 3	25% 40%
NISEC	9	30%
SEG	4	25%
WJEC	4	30%

Figure 12   Coursework models in relation to weighting

In Figure 13 (below) we look at the objectives that can be assessed within different tasks. It is possible to assess more than one objective within a task, so teachers will need to be aware of the requirements of their particular syllabus.

As a further *aide-mémoire* we list in Figure 14 (below) many of the actual words that can be used within the context of each of the three different assessment objectives.

Assessment objective K U E	Examples
* *	**Test** on the Parable of the Good Samaritan
* *	**Unseen written paper** checking dates of festivals
* * *	**Essay** on the Ten Gurus
* * *	**Visual** Look at slides of paintings of the crucifixion and comment on the religious symbolism
* * *	**Text** Read and explain the meaning of two suras and give your opinion of them
* *	**Letter** Write a letter containing your experiences about a pilgrimage you have just been on
* * *	**Visit** Observe an initiation ceremony and consider its value for the community
* *	**Research** and write about the main events in the life and work of Mother Teresa
* *	**Review** the film *Gandhi*

Figure 13   Identifying assessment objectives K/U/E in tasks

K	U	E
Construct	Explain the meaning	What do you think?
Select	Explain the significance	Give your opinion
State	Explain the purpose	Say with reasons
Imagine	Explain why	Consider
Describe	Explain the importance	Is this of benefit?
Investigate	Comment upon	What criticisms?
Write an account	Show how	Should?
Describe	Why?	What is the value?

Figure 14

Fairer assessment?

The General Criteria state that teachers are in the best position to judge the merits of their students in relation to each other. The coursework component will bring assessment back into the classroom, being based on several pieces of work over two years, rather than on two timed written examinations. It remains to be seen whether this will facilitate fairer assessment.

Coursework assessment will involve teachers in:

(a) collecting information – devising and setting students' assignments;
(b) relating coursework tasks to assessment criteria;
(c) interpreting the results – giving regular feedback to students;
(d) gathering information – systematic record-keeping and monitoring;
(e) evaluating tasks, teaching and assessment practices.

Activity 11 What are you currently assessing?

Fill in the chart (Figure 15, below) and use the information contained in this chapter to evaluate what objective you are currently assessing within the tasks you set in Religious Education/Studies in your school.

Knowledge *'The what?'*
Understanding *'The why then?'*
Evaluation *'The so what?'*

Figure 15

Activity 12 Changes and implications?

1 What implications will the coursework component of your chosen syllabus have for your teaching and classroom organisation?
2 Will you need to change the emphasis of your teaching to encourage students to develop a critical approach to the subject? How will you do this?

2

The role of the teacher within assessment

Within coursework assessment, increased responsibility for student assessment is given to the teacher. GCSE aims to reform current assessment procedures in public examinations. However, this reform may only be realised through teachers. What are the new roles that teachers will have to take on? This chapter looks more closely at the roles involved and suggests that any change must build upon aspects of good teaching practice currently used in the classroom.

Few teachers of Religious Studies will find the underlying philosophy of GCSE either new or alien, though many may be fearful of the practical, organisational and administrative aspects involved in devising and examining coursework. We discuss how teachers involved in this 'pioneering' phase can be encouraged and supported to develop their skills and confidence in order to undertake their formal assessment role.

The major changes being introduced within GCSE are coursework and differentiation. We have already noted that coursework will involve assessing and recording the normal outcome of classroom activities in a systematic way. With regard to coursework assessment, the relationship between teachers and students is complicated. The overall role of the teacher is outlined in Figure 16 (below).

CREATE	Teachers must create all coursework tasks in relation to the full ability range and provide varied tasks covering the syllabus allowing objectives to be assessed
KNOW	Teachers must know the ability range and capability of each student to encourage positive achievement
DEVELOP	Teachers must develop appropriate marking schemes and ensure that students are aware of the demands and their implications
PLAN	Teachers must plan coursework in relation to timing, frequency, number, and completion dates
MARK, MONITOR RECORD	Teachers must mark, monitor and record coursework tasks, document the nature of assistance given to students and, where practicable, include student-evaluation.

Figure 16   Teacher involvement in coursework

Teacher guidance and supervision

Teacher guidance and supervision is essential if coursework is to be both a teaching, as well as an assessment, strategy. However, teachers face a delicate problem in working out the nature and extent to which they can support students in carrying out their coursework assignments. Teachers have responsibility as *advisers*, but what might this include? All candidates should be enabled to acquire and apply religious knowledge and understanding, thus teachers must provide students with opportunities to develop and demonstrate their skills and achievements.

Teachers would normally undertake the following tasks:

(a) preparing students to undertake assignment;
(b) where there is choice, giving guidance appropriate to the levels of ability;
(c) giving guidance as to the nature of difficulty and sources available;
(d) suggesting further developments, approaches and areas of possible enquiry;
(e) supervising of work so as to prevent plagiarism, monitoring progress and ensuring that the appropriate proportion of time is spent;
(f) encouraging students to use their critical faculties to give thoughtful personal responses;
(g) advising students about the presentation or format of final assignment and ensuring that work is completed according to syllabus requirements.

It is worth noting a few general principles which arise from this.

1 Teacher-guidance must not be denied to students merely because the piece of work undertaken is to form part of an assignment.
2 Teachers must try to ensure that guidance must not direct, or correct, to an extent that it alters the individual nature of the assignment.
3 Teacher-supervision need not be restricted to monitoring students' activities but can include advice and suggestions.
4 Examining groups will generally request that teachers and students sign the assessment record form to declare that the work has been undertaken according to conditions acceptable to the Group.

Some problems discussed   A number of the problems involved in the assessment to be performed by teachers are shown in Figure 17 (below).

How is an
individual within collaborative
group work assessed?

What level of teacher-
assistance is appropriate
in arranging for a visit
to a place of worship?

Can practical/creative
work (models, artefacts, drawings)
be assessed?

PROBLEMS
OR
POSSIBILITIES?

Can assessment be made
of achievements for which
there is transitory evidence
(e.g. a performance of a Hindu dance
or ritual of Muslim prayer)?

How can oral work
such as a recorded interview
or discussion be assessed?

Figure 17

These problems may be addressed by specifying:

(a) which assessment objective is being assessed;
(b) what will be accepted as evidence that a student has attained a particular goal;

(c) how marks are to be allocated for each achievement (i.e. a comprehensive mark scheme is required).

The nature of the teacher-assistance must be built into the scheme, which must also be flexible enough to take on board the unexpected.

Assessing an individual's contribution within group work

Where Examining Groups allow group coursework to be submitted, teachers must ensure than an individual student's contribution can be identified and has been assessed separately. They must also ensure that they do not direct, or correct, in such a way that the nature of students' work within a group is drastically changed.

It is worth looking carefully at the information provided by Examining Groups concerning coursework. All Groups agree that the major teaching-role is in guiding students. Teachers may thus support and advise students on their choice of topic (taking note of their preferences) and brief them about the suitability of source material and research methods.

What students need to know

Whether students are working independently on an assignment, or as part of a group, they will need to understand fully what is required of them. Structuring tasks clearly will help, though additionally teachers will have to structure lessons to make time for individual tutorials concerning mark-weightings, length of work and time-limits. Students may also find it helpful if teachers explain or describe what the tasks will look like as finished products.

Where assignments require basic study skills such as how to write a letter, or manual skills such as how to use a tape-recorder or camera, teachers must make sure that students actually possess these skills. It is worth emphasising the importance of ensuring that tasks carry the same meaning for students across the whole ability range. Attention is needed over the language (vocabulary and structure); the form; the implied conventions; the implied skills; and the intelligibility of the instructions whether spoken or written.

Coursework folder requirements

The content, presentation and submission of a coursework folder will depend upon the syllabus and Examining Group you have chosen. However, the following general points emerge in relation to Religious Studies coursework.

1 Coursework assignments should be presented or documented on A4 paper.
2 Credit will not be given for dictated notes.
3 Coursework consisting solely of scrapbook material, photographs, newspaper or magazine cuttings will gain little credit.
4 A variety of work may be submitted.
5 Teacher assistance must reflect that which is acceptable under the scheme of assessment.
6 It is assumed that the pieces of work selected should represent the student's best work.
7 The folder should not be produced under formal examination conditions, though work such as timed essays and class tests may be submitted.
8 Coursework may be completed at home or in class.
9 Candidates may produce coursework with or without teacher discussion or guidance.
10 Each piece of work must be accompanied by a description of the conditions under which it has been produced.

11 Each piece of work submitted must appear on the final mark sheet.

12 The entire folder must be available for moderation if requested by the Examining Group.

Feedback to students

Setting coursework assignments which are then marked and assessed, gives teachers direct student feedback. Such feedback is particularly important to ensure that differentiation has taken place. Student-feedback may come in a variety of forms and teachers will be in the best position to judge how best it can be utilised in their own situation.

Teachers' remuneration for assessment

The whole issue of teachers' pay for assessment work is still a very sore issue when taking stock of the increased demands from the Examining Groups. Such issues cannot be fully discussed here because they are bound up with what constitutes teachers' 'normal' duties. It is worth noting, however, that the Joint Council has issued a statement to the effect that Examining Groups should pay 'an appropriate rate for the job', though they declined to state what this might be.

Activity 13 Self-evaluation

GCSE will require teachers to be familiar with monitoring, evaluation and assessment techniques. Self-evaluation is an important tool in helping to measure the effectiveness of what is taught and can be used to improve the quality of students' learning experiences.

1 Use the six questions in Figure 18 (below) to evaluate one of your lessons.

2 How could you use or adapt this method to: (a) assess an individual within a group; (b) monitor a whole group?

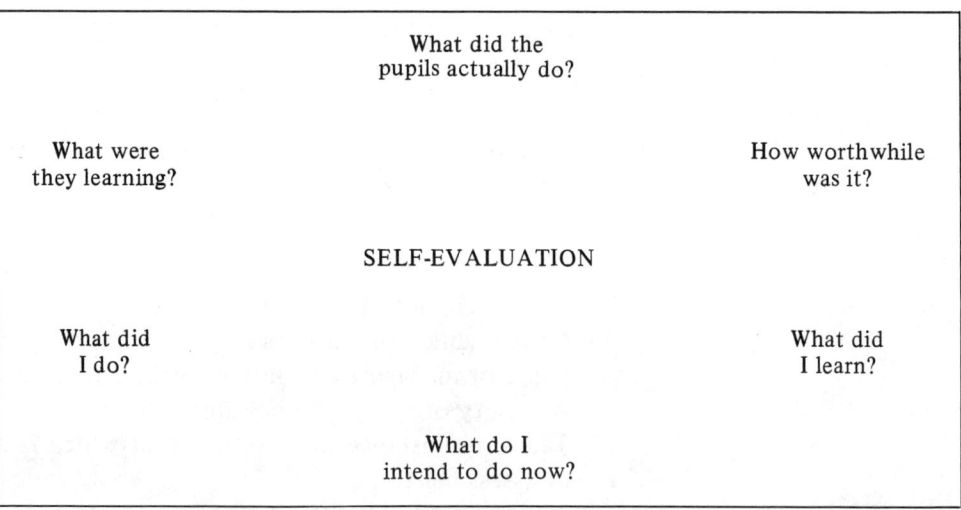

Figure 18 Evaluation developed by the Open University Curriculum in Action team, and quoted here from the Hargreaves Report (ILEA 1985 4.6.2)

Activity 14 Problems and possibilities

Look at Figure 17 (page 58) and consider whether each statement represents a problem or a possibility within the assessment process.

---

3   Assessing to criteria

The notion of criterion-referenced grading is central to GCSE. We have already noted that criterion-referenced grading describes a system in which grades are awarded according to a series of pre-determined standards. The introduction of grade criteria within GCSE represents a major shift away from norm-referencing (used in GCE and CSE examinations) in which students are graded in relation to the performance of other students entered for the same examination.

Figure 19 (below) shows how GCSE grades relate to GCE and CSE grades.

GCE O-level	GCSE	CSE
A	A	
B	B	1
C	C	
D	D	2
E	E	3
	F	4
	G	5

Figure 19 How GCSE grades relate to GCE and CSE grades

Grade Criteria and Grade Descriptions

Within GCSE, Grade Criteria are explicit statements of what candidates have to achieve in order to be awarded a particular grade. The task of producing Grade Criteria requires careful setting of levels of achievement to match certain grades. When complete, they will represent the measurement of achievement in 'absolute' terms. Grade Criteria will clarify educational targets and facilitate the construction of achievement and educational standards. These criteria are currently being developed and exist only in draft form. For the first GCSE examination, Examining Groups will rely upon 'Grade Descriptions'.

Grade Descriptions give a general indication of the standards of achievement likely to have been shown by the candidate awarded a particular grade. The grade awarded will depend, in practice, upon the extent to which the candidate has met the overall assessment objectives and it may conceal weakness in one aspect which is balanced by above-average performance in some other.

Examining Groups specify descriptions of grades from the point of view of the assessment objectives. Assessing to criteria means that candidates are assessed according to what they have positively achieved and shown that they 'can do' as indicated in Figure 20 (page 62).

Each of the Examining Groups give descriptions, based upon the National Criteria, of what they consider candidates awarded Grades A, C and F should have achieved. In Figure 21 (page 62) we summarise these to illustrate the basic differences between Grade Descriptions.

To look at this another way, we show in more detail in Figure 22 (page 62) what a Grade A candidate is expected to have achieved within the three assessment objectives.

61

> *Assessing to criteria*
> *Candidates are assessed on*
> Their knowledge of the content of syllabus
> Their ability to select and present information
> Their ability to organise information
> Their ability to show their understanding
> Their ability to evaluate or express an opinion

Figure 20   Grade Descriptions are based on assessment objectives

	Grade F	*Grade C*	*Grade A*
Knowledge of content	partial	wide	thorough
Selection of information	some/relevant	some/salient	several/salient
Organisation of ideas	show an attempt	show some skill	show maturity
Understanding	in some area	a reasonable	a thorough
Ability to evaluate/ express opinions	clearly	using evidence	use evidence and argument

Figure 21   Summarising Grade Descriptions

> 1 Show clear knowledge of a range of facts and can present and select relevant information.
> 2 Show extensive understanding of the language, terms and concepts used in religion; the role and importance in religion of special people, writing and traditions; principal beliefs of the religion or religions being studied, the meanings given to those beliefs by adherents and the ways in which beliefs are related to the personal and corporate practice of religion; religious and, where appropriate, non-religious responses to contemporary moral issues both personal and social; questions about the meaning of life and the variety of faith-responses which may be given to them.
> 3 Show an ability to evaluate a wide range of evidence and/or opinion with sensitivity, precision and balance.

Figure 22   An example of what a Grade A candidate should achieve from NISEC

Marking schemes

We have noted that, for many teachers, coursework will represent their first opportunity to contribute to formal assessment. It is important to draw teachers' attention to the fact that just as task-setting must relate to how far students have achieved the objectives, marking must also do this. Thus teachers must devise mark-schemes alongside their students' assignments. Simply expressed, a mark-scheme outlines precisely how marks are allocated and distributed for a piece of coursework.

Marking

When marking work in Religious Studies, teachers might first attempt to gain an impression of the standard of the work before deciding whether it has fulfilled the criteria for assessment. There are both strengths and weaknesses in approaching marking in this way.

In general the teacher must aim to create schemes which indicate how marks are to be allocated, but are flexible enough so as to not be over-prescriptive.

For example, if the question was 'Briefly describe the Ka'aba', the mark-scheme should give an indication of what would be accepted as an answer. If the mark-scheme was prescriptive it might suggest that the only specific answer would be to say that the Ka'aba is in Mecca and that it is cube-shaped. Applied rigidly, this scheme is unlikely to credit students giving an alternative answer that the Ka'aba is covered with a black cloth called the Kiswah and that it has a sacred black stone. Whilst setting out, as far as possible, how marks are to be allocated it is necessary to indicate in the mark scheme that unexpected answers and responses will not be penalised.

When applied to the marking of coursework designed to allow candidates to express personal opinions and evaluations, it is even more important to allow for a wide variety of responses. Teachers must be careful to use their discretion and always to reward positive achievement. The shift in GCSE is that teachers are required to look for and mark what students 'can do'. Teachers should be looking for strengths, merits and students' positive achievement in order to ensure differentiation by outcome.

Assessment models

Examining Groups give details of how teachers are required to assess each of the assignments according to their own model or pattern. It is useful to refer to examples of these before moving on to look at documentation.

The SEG requires teachers to assess each of four assignments according to the pattern shown in Figure 23 (below). Each piece is marked out of 25 marks and these are allocated in the way shown, in relation to the objectives.

Factual knowledge	5 marks
Understanding	15 marks
Evaluation	5 marks

Figure 23 SEG assessment model

The MEG provide teachers with a detailed grid which generally indicates how they should allocate marks within each grade according to the weighting of the objectives in coursework. This is shown in Figure 24 (below).

	Mark range available for each objective		
GCSE Grade	*Knowledge*	*Understanding*	*Evaluation*
A	12–13	18–20	16–17
B	10–11	15–17	13–15
C	8–9	12–14	11–12
D	6–7	10–11	8–10
E	5–6	7–9	6–7
F	3–4	4–6	3–5
G	1–2	1–3	

Figure 24 Example of mark-scheme from the MEG, based on syllabus C

Devising mark-schemes requires planning, and teachers will need to ensure not only that marking schemes are fair, but also that they reflect the differentiation within the task. Teaching an objectives-led course demands that, in addition to factual recall, different levels of understanding, evaluation and thoughtful responses are also assessed and this must somehow be reflected within the mark scheme. Setting-out mark-schemes allows teachers to evaluate whether the tasks they have set are realistic and provide students with an opportunity to demonstrate the objectives.

Teachers are required to maintain careful records of marks awarded to each student on each assignment and to ensure that all coursework, including mark schemes, are available for moderation. In the following chapters we shall look more closely at these aspects of the assessment process.

Activity 15 Grading

1 In your opinion does the grading system within your Examining Group and chosen syllabus provide you with sufficient guidelines to convince you about the shift in emphasis from norm-based assessment to criterion-referencing?
2 Do you consider that in trying to make the criteria watertight, an unworkable model has been produced?
3 Do you consider that in trying to make the criteria 'user-friendly' the criteria (descriptions) have been reduced to generalities?

Activity 16 Marking schemes

1 What do you consider to be the major strengths and weaknesses of a firmly structured marking scheme?
2 Is it possible to devise a mark-scheme based on, for example, a neutral stimulus which effectively differentiates by outcome?

4   Organising for assessment

Points for planning

We have noted previously that teachers must consider several related points which make up the assessment process. These are represented in Figure 25 (below).

```
┌─────────────────────────────────────────────────────────────┐
│                    Timing of assessment                      │
│                                                              │
│                      POINTS TO                               │
│                      CONSIDER                                │
│  Relating tasks                                              │
│  to objectives                                               │
│                                              Defining tasks  │
│                                                              │
│                   Devising mark scheme                       │
└─────────────────────────────────────────────────────────────┘
```

Figure 25

Recording assessments

The coursework folder and classroom evaluation have not previously been closely related to the assessment process within Religious Studies. Helping teachers and students document their work is an important feature of the new examination. A fundamental principle underlying coursework preparation for teachers and students is the need for planning. A careful account must be kept of each student's work, the nature and type of teacher-assistance, as well as the mark sheets for coursework assignments. Teachers may therefore find it necessary to keep a full record (or profile) of all work completed by students throughout the duration of the course. Students' self-assessment should also form part of such a profile.

Teachers of Religious Studies will need to develop and adapt mark-schemes for coursework assessment which suit their particular situation and needs. Consideration must be given to what is actually recorded and to its form and presentation.

Profiles

Teachers use a variety of methods to record students' progress in their subject, the most common being the 'mark book'. However, not all teachers or departments have clear ideas about marking policies. Profiling attempts to maintain an ongoing record of students' achievement. A profile is an important instrument in helping teachers assess students' ability in both the affective and cognitive domains. If done throughout schooling, it should form an integral part of the whole learning process informing teachers, parents and students. Put very simply, a profile is a device for recording information derived from assessment. It is not, in itself, a method of assessment, but a concrete statement of what students have achieved. Profiles record success rather than failure and actively involve students in the process.

Profiles and GCSE Religious Studies

Whilst there is no direct link yet between GCSE coursework and student profiles, there is no reason why the two should not be complementary. Used alongside the coursework folder, a profile could be used to inform teachers' grading decisions at the end of the course. When entering students for examination courses and making other important decisions concerning their ability and standard, such a record is extremely useful. Five points emerge as having implications for teachers attempting to develop a systematic approach to profiling for GCSE:

(a) the need for cumulative assessment;
(b) the role of personal judgement;
(c) the need to identify specific skills and ways of monitoring them;
(d) the need for a variety of assessment instruments;
(e) assessment should as far as possible include student self-assessment.

Recording the nature of teacher assistance

It is advisable that teachers maintain rigorous notes and records on the nature of any assistance given to an individual student and it may be helpful to devise school-based marking or record sheets. Figure 26 (page 67) is an example of one Religious Studies Department's attempt to devise a mark/assessment sheet in relation to coursework assignments. It is worth noting that whilst this particular assessment record sheet may have limitations, it can be used in the following ways:

(a) to maintain an accurate record of teacher guidance and supervision;
(b) to identify which assessment objective is being assessed;
(c) to allow the separate or combined assessment of objectives;
(d) to acknowledge differentiation within different tasks;
(e) to authenticate assignment as the student's own work;
(f) to involve student in the assessment process in a climate of negotiation;
(g) to acknowledge student feedback seriously;
(h) to provide a back-up for profiles or report-writing;
(i) to use as guidance and feedback for parents.

Coursework record and marking sheets

Each Examining Group gives concise guidance on the format of the records of assessments for coursework. To show the possibility of different styles and formats, Figures 27 (page 68) and 28 (page 69) offer two examples of different record sheets, together with comments. The examples may also be a useful stimulus for those teachers wishing to create their own record-keeping scheme.

The first example (Figure 27, page 68) is based on the WJEC coursework component. This consists of four assignments which together account for 30% of the total examination mark.

For each assignment, teachers make clear the weighting of marks given for each assessment objective tested, and the marks gained by the students for these objectives. Assignments set need not test all three assessment objectives. In any assignment only those assessment objectives tested should be recorded. In this scheme the maximum mark available for any one assignment is 30 marks. Four assignments carry a maximum of 120 marks which is divided by four to give the final total.

********** SCHOOL DEPARTMENT OF RELIGIOUS STUDIES

COURSEWORK ASSESSMENT SHEET

Student's name _____

Title of assignment _____

Nature/type of assignment:

Classwork _____ Homework _____ Home/Classwork _____ Test _____

Assessment objective(s): Knowledge _____ Understanding _____ Evaluation _____

Max. mark(s)   _____   _____   _____

Nature of teacher assistance:

Teacher comment:

                                                                Initial mark: _____

Student comment:

                                                                Signed:
                                                                Date:

Additional comments:

                                                                Final mark: _____
                                                                Signed:
                                                                Date:

Figure 26   An attempt to devise a simple, clear record and marking sheet

The second example (Figure 28, page 69) is taken from the SEG syllabus. Students examined by SEG are required to submit four assignments of about a thousand words each and based on the content of the syllabus. Each piece of coursework must include all assessment objectives.

Several important points emerge from looking at these examples of record- and mark-sheets.

1 It is vital that the marking is related to the assessment objectives.
2 Each Examining Group requires objectives to be assessed and recorded differently.
3 There is a need to draw up a marking scheme when setting the assignment.
4 Everyone involved must know on what basis marks are awarded.
5 The scheme of assessment must stand up to external moderation.

Whatever form the coursework takes, a fundamental principle is the necessity for careful planning and maintenance of accurate records.

**RELIGIOUS STUDIES
COURSEWORK RECORD SHEET**

Centre _____ Centre No. _____

Candidate's name _____ Candidate's No. _____

Assignment Option Date Title of coursework	Marks awarded Assessment objectives				Office use
	3.1	3.2	3.3	Total	
1					/30
2					/30
3					/30
4					/30
Total	/40	/40	/40	/120	
			Final total =	/30	

Figure 27

COURSEWORK MARK SHEET

Candidate's name _____   Number _____

School _____   Syllabus A/B/C_____

TITLE OF COURSEWORK

APPROVED   DATE

BIBLIOGRAPHY

OTHER SOURCES

Teacher's assessment	Maximum marks	Initital marks per piece 1 2 3 4	For use by Group only Moderated marks
1 Factual knowledge	5		
2 Understanding	15		
3 Evaluation	5		
Divide by 4 to give final total %	Marks total		

Signed ....
Initial marker   ....
                                        Moderator

Figure 28

Activity 17 Marking and recording

1 List all the methods you currently use to mark and assess work for Religious Education/Studies (common-core or examination).
2 What methods do you currently use to record your assessments?
3 It will be important to keep a record of the amount of time and guidance you give to your students to ensure accurate assessments can be made. How do you propose to do this?

Activity 18 Assessment and record-sheets

1 Look at Figure 26 (page 67) and discuss what the merits and shortcomings of the form might be.
2 Use your criticisms to build up an assessment/profile to suit your particular needs.

5   Moderation: who does what and when?

What is moderation?

Coursework assessment depends heavily upon the professionalism of teachers. Assessment criteria are included in all syllabuses to ensure that this is done fairly and some Groups also include 'marking schemes'. Moderation ensures that assessment between centres is standardised, without bias or malpractice. Coursework is internally assessed and externally moderated. Teachers are usually responsible for standardising the marking of coursework in their individual centres. Moderation, the regulation of marks and grades within a whole Examining Group, is the responsibility of that Examining Group and is usually undertaken by appointed Moderators and Assessors.

Moderation ensures that:

(a) there are no variations in standards across the Examining Group;
(b) all candidates are treated fairly.

Who are the moderators?

They are either:

(a) examiners appointed by Examining Groups who re-mark the coursework (and consequently give little feedback to teachers);
(b) teachers who meet to reach a consensus on standards (and in the process acquire some in-service training);
(c) accredited teachers. Currently one Examining Group is working towards the introduction of a system where teachers have an opportunity to become 'Accredited', i.e. not needing to have their assessments subjected to formal moderation. An accredited teacher would be given autonomy to plan, implement and assess his/her own coursework. Such a scheme rests upon the assumption that teachers possess not only professional expertise but also the integrity to carry out the assessment without external scrutiny.

Some Examining Groups have appointed Assessors and Moderators whilst others will hold Consensus Meetings. Others may choose to use both in order to gain further experience. Examining Groups reserve the right to request further information from centres. They are responsible for guiding teachers about assessment and the moderation process. Further, as the coursework component is relatively new in this subject area, the moderation procedure may itself be subject to moderation by the Examining Groups in the light of experience.

How will moderation be carried out?

Most commonly, moderation is performed by means of statistical or sampling methods.

Statistical moderation

In Religious Studies the objectives assessed in the coursework are the same as those assessed in the written paper(s), though there is a slight difference in their overall weighting. It is possible, therefore, that some Examining Groups may use statistical moderation to adjust for the differences in standards between different centres (or assessment sets).

In this process the written paper becomes the 'moderating instrument'. An objective measure of the candidate's attainment is gained using his/her performance in the written paper. This objective measure is then used as a screening device. Only if there is some variation in the overall performance of a group of candidates between the coursework and written paper is an adjustment made to the internal marks. It is not the individual's performances between the two components which are compared, but the group performances of all candidates in an assessment set.

The scaled mean of the marks for the written paper (the moderating instrument) is compared with the mean of the marks for the internally assessed component. If there is a difference between the two, over and above the 'allowed difference', the marks are adjusted. Statistical moderation is not applied in a purely mechanical way. Provision is made for moderated marks to be scrutinised and examiners can intercede where this procedure is seen to operate unfairly.

Moderation by inspection sampling

Coursework marks can also be moderated by inspecting samples of candidates' completed assignments. Centres will be required to submit mark-sheets to the Group, and samples of candidates' work will be selected from these and inspected for moderation purposes. The sample will usually ensure that examples of candidates' work cover the whole ability-range in that centre. Where centres have small numbers, usually all the work will be requested.

Figure 29 (below) indicates the preferences of the different Examining Groups.

EXAM GROUP	*MODERATION*			
	Inspection		*Statistical*	*Dependent upon*
	(Ext. Mod.)	*(Consortium)*		*local considerations*
LEAG	*			
MEG	*	*	*	*
NEA		*	*	
NISEC				*
SEG	*	*		
WJEC				*

Figure 29 Examining Groups' likely moderation models

Implications for teachers

There are three main implications which arise out of the process of moderation.

1 Teachers will need to consider the internal moderation arrangements for their department in order to establish uniform standards within the department. For those teachers of Religious Studies who are on their own, they will need to consider how they might liaise with colleagues from other departments in other schools so as to discuss regularly coursework tasks, assessment schemes and monitor moderation.

2 Teachers must ensure that the activities chosen for assessment purposes satisfy the requirements of the Examining Group with regard to the scheme of moderation to be used.

3 Teachers should realise that the major importance of teacher assessment is ensuring that the students are placed in the correct order of achievement.

Activity 19 Syllabus choice

For those teachers who have chosen their syllabus on the basis of the course-work model rather than the coursework demands, have your attitudes and opinions been shaped by your reading?

Activity 20 Reviewing your stiuation

1 Make a list of the most significant changes that GCSE will have on you and your department.
2 What strategies and solutions have you devised to adapt to the new situation?

Appendix: The Examining Groups

The purpose of this appendix is to draw attention to the assessment criteria and grading system within each of the Examining Groups.

The syllabuses, with coursework weighting from each of the Examining Groups, appear in alphabetical order.

LONDON AND EAST ANGLIA GROUP

Syllabus A: Thematic Study of Judaism, Christianity and Islam

Syllabus B: Two from following eleven units to be studied
      1 Buddhism
      2 Christianity
      3 Hinduism
      4 Islam
      5 Judaism
      6 Sikhism
      7 Personal and Social Issues: Family and Community Life
      8 Personal and Social Issues: Social Order and Material World
      9 Religious Texts of Christian Tradition: The Bible
     10 Religious Texts of Christian Tradition: St Mark's Gospel
     11 Religious Texts of Jewish Tradition: The Bible and Post-Biblical

---

Syllabus A:	One Paper (2½ hr) 60%	Ten pieces of coursework 40%
Syllabus B:	One Paper (2½ hr) 60%	Ten pieces of coursework (Five from each section) 40%

MIDLAND EXAMINING GROUP

Syllabus A:	Any two of the following sections
	1 A Christian Sacred Text: St Luke's Gospel
	2 Christian Perspectives on Personal and Social Issues
	3 Christianity
	4 Hinduism
	5 Islam
	6 Judaism
	7 Sikhism
Syllabus B:	Thematic Study of three from following religions
	Christianity, Hinduism, Islam, Judaism and Sikhism
	Section 1: Encounter with Religions (compulsory)
	Section 2: Religious Practices *or*
	Section 3: Religion in the Everyday World
Syllabus C:	Section 1: Belief and Practice of Christians according to New Testament
	Section 2: Christian Belief and Practice in the Modern World

Syllabus A:	Two Papers, with each including questions from both sections
	Paper 1: 1½ hr 32% Paper 2: 2½ hr 48%
	Coursework: Three pieces (at least one from each section) 20%
Syllabus B:	Section 1: One Paper 2½ hr 60%
	Either Section 2: One Paper 50 mins 20% + Two pieces of coursework 20%
	Or Section 3: No paper but Six pieces of coursework 40%
Syllabus C:	Section 1: One Paper 2½ hr 40% + Coursework: Two pieces 15%
	Section 2: One paper 1½ hr 30% + Coursework: Two pieces 15%

NORTHERN EXAMINING ASSOCIATION

Syllabus A:	Dimensions of Religion – choose two options
	Option 1 Buddhism *or* The Person and Ministry of Jesus (St Mark's Gospel)
	Option 2 a) Christianity *or* b) Aspects of Christian Life (Roman Catholicism)
	Option 3 Hinduism
	Option 4 Islam
	Option 5 Judaism
	Option 6 a) Sikhism *or* b) Contemporary Issues in Christian Perspectives
	(2b and 6b cannot be taken simultaneously)
Syllabus B:	Themes from three world religions
	Part One: Buddhism; Hinduism; Sikhism
	Part Two: Christianity; Islam and Judaism

Syllabus A:	Two Papers, one on each option of 1¾ hr 75%
	Coursework: One long or three short pieces for each option 25%
Syllabus B:	One Paper 2¼ hr 60%
	Coursework: Three pieces on areas not examined in paper 40%

NORTHERN IRELAND SCHOOLS EXAMINATIONS COUNCIL

Option A: All take 1 and 2 and either 3 or 4
             1 Focus on Jesus through Law, Prophets, Promise and Community
             2 The Church in the Modern World: Its Life and Practice
             3 Marriage, Home and Family: Christian Perspective and Response
             4 Service for Others/Who is my Neighbour?

Option B: 1 Focus on Jesus through Law, Prophets, Promise and Community
             2 Another Pattern of Belief – choose one of following
               a) Hinduism
               b) Judaism
               c) Islam

Option A: One Common Paper 2½ hr 70% (C to G)
             Or Common Paper 35% + Optional Extension Paper 1½ hr 35% (A to G)
             Coursework: Nine pieces on set themes 30%

Option B: One Common Paper 2½ hr 70%
             Or Common Paper 35% + Optional Extension Paper 1½ hr 35% (A to G)
             Coursework: Nine pieces on set themes 30%

SOUTHERN EXAMINING GROUP

Syllabus A: Any two of the following
              Buddhism; Islam; Jesus in the Synoptic Gospels; Christianity; Judaism;
              Christian Perspectives on Contemporary Issues; Hinduism; Sikhism

Syllabus B: Personal and Social Ethics in a Multi-Faith Context
              Three themes of   a) Marriage and the Family
                              b) Peace and Conflict
                              c) Humankind and Nature
              studied in relation to Christianity; Hinduism; Islam and secular response

Syllabus C: Thematic Study of any three religions from
              Buddhism; Christianity; Hinduism; Islam; Judaism and Sikhism

Syllabus A: Two papers, each with questions from both sections
              Paper 1 1½ hr 35%   Paper 2 1¾ hr 40%
              Coursework: Four pieces (two on each section) 25%

Syllabus B: Two papers, each with questions from whole syllabus
              Paper 1 1½ hr 35%   Paper 2 1¾ hr 40%
              Coursework: Four pieces one on each theme; one biographical 25%

Syllabus C: As for A and B

WELSH JOINT EDUCATIONAL COMMITTEE

Nine options are in three groups. Candidates must study one option from each of any two groups: (E and H may not be taken together)

Group 1:   A: Foundation and Teaching of Christianity
E: A Christian Understanding of the Old Testament
I: Islam

Group 2:   B: Discovering the Church and its Mission
F: Hinduism
H: Judaism

Group 3:   C: Christian Celebrations, Festivals and Movements
D: Christianity and Contemporary Society
G: Buddhism

Two papers, one on each option 1½ hr 35% each
Coursework: Four pieces, two from each option 30%

Conclusion

This book has aimed to reflect the concern that teachers will have as they take on board the objectives underlying the GCSE examination. We have attempted to highlight the shift in emphasis that is required to encourage 'Understanding' and 'the ability to Evaluate' within Religious Studies.

In our opinion the inclusion of coursework represents a hard-won development within the educational thinking of Examining Groups. As a concept, and perhaps a reality within the classroom, coursework must be nurtured and protected by those teaching Religious Studies, particularly if it is to escape the limitations of norm-referenced assessment.

This book supports teachers by providing practical examples of coursework and sufficient background knowledge of GCSE to enable them to make a reasonable start on the teaching of their chosen syllabus. It will be through only the continued energy and resourcefulness of the already over-burdened teacher that we can keep assessment where it belongs – *in the classroom*!

Bibliography

Blake, C. 'GCSE under starter's orders' *RE Today*, Autumn 1986

Burke, P. 'Putting teachers back in charge' *The Times Educational Supplement*, 26.9.86

C.E.M. *R.E. Professional Papers 3: current issues in examinations*, 1981

Clare, J. 'The Revolution that isn't' *The Listener*, 18.9.86

Department of Education and Science/Welsh Office *General Certificate of Secondary Education: a general introduction*, HMSO, 1985

Department of Education and Science/Welsh Office *The National Criteria: religious studies*, 1985

Department of Education and Science *Records of Personal Achievement for School-leavers. A Draft Policy Statement*, 1983

Kingdom, M. & Stobart, G. 'GCSE: Accentuating the Positive' *Education*, 29.8.86

Leech, A. 'The Professionals' anxieties' *Education*, 7.2.86

Lupton, H. 'Checklists for the Study of RE Syllabuses' *Learning for Living*, Spring 1975

Mills, I. 'Evaluating Different Religious Traditions' *Learning for Living*, Autumn 1976

Murphy, R. 'A Revolution in Educational Assessment?' *Forum* Vol. 28 No 2, 1986

Secondary Examinations Council *Working Paper 1: Differentiated Assessment in GCSE*, 1985

Secondary Examinations Council *Working Paper 2: Coursework Assessment in GCSE*, 1985

Secondary Examinations Council/BBC Broadcasting Support Services *A Guide to the GCSE*, 1986

Secondary Examinations Council/Open University *Religious Studies GCSE: a guide for teachers*, 1986

Wood, A. *Assessment in a Multicultural Society: Religious Studies at 16+*, Longman/Schools Council, 1984